THE PATTERN

Discovering God's Design for Marriage

dev menon

THE PATTERN
Copyright © 2015 Dev Menon

All rights reserved. No part of this publication may be reproduced, stored in a retrieval system, or transmitted, in any form or by any means, electronic, mechanical, photocopying, recording or otherwise, without the prior written permission of the author, except in the case of brief quotations embodied in critical articles and reviews.

Published by Graceworks Pte Ltd
22 Sin Ming Lane
#04-76 Midview City
Singapore 573969
Email: enquiries@graceworks.com.sg
Website: www.graceworks.com.sg

Scripture quotations are taken from The Holy Bible, English Standard Version®. Copyright © 2001 by Crossway Bibles, a division of Good News Publishers. All rights reserved.

A CIP record for this book is available from the National Library Board, Singapore.

Design by Intent Design

ISBN: 978-981-09-5476-5

Printed in Singapore

1 2 3 4 5 6 7 8 9 10 . 24 23 22 21 20 19 18 17 16 15

CONTENTS

	Foreword	v
	Acknowledgements	vii
1.	Things Change	1
2.	The 113 Pattern	11
3.	Rules of Engagement	17
4.	When Two Become One (I)	37
5.	When Two Become One (II)	51
6.	A Dance for Two	75
7.	The Final Word	101
8.	A Summary	107
	Appendix A: Conflict Resolution	109
	Appendix B: Maybe Not?	113
	Endnotes	115

FOREWORD

I witness every wedding with mixed feelings. There is much joy as two people in love commit themselves to each other, and there is the joyful anticipation of how the marriage can become a blessing to the couple and to others. But there is also a degree of apprehension as even the best of marriages need hard work to succeed and too many marriages don't work out even among followers of Jesus.

Couples need help as they embark on their life together, which is why we welcome this book on marriage preparation by Rev Dr Dev Menon. He brings all the right qualifications to the job. He is a pastor who has done marriage preparation for many couples, he has studied theology, and perhaps most important of all, he is married with three children.

Of all the marriage preparation books I have seen, *The Pattern* is the most theological. First, he takes seriously the fact that humankind is made in God's image, and therefore marriage must take seriously the nature of God, especially the relationships between the three members of the Trinity. Dev draws out the implications of the relationships between Father, Son and Spirit for the relationship between a husband and a wife. He does this creatively but always with fidelity to the Bible.

Second, Dev makes it very clear that marriage cannot work without God's help. God sets a high bar for marriage. A marriage can only work if the partners have first tasted the love of God. Only then are they able to love each other as God intended. Indeed, "we love because He first loved us" (1 John 4:19).

And when a marriage works as intended by God, it gives the world a glimpse of the reality and character of God. A good marriage is both a blessing to the couple and serves to reveal the living God to the world.

Readers will find Dev's writing conversational and accessible. He combines a strong theological framework with a lot of practical help for couples as they begin their marriage. While those preparing for marriage need counsellors, mentors, and models – companions who will walk with them – they also need to base their marriage on God and His truth. *The Pattern* provides this biblical foundation and does it admirably.

Rev Dr Tan Soo Inn
Director
Graceworks

ACKNOWLEDGEMENTS

To my wife Chene, who still amazes me after eight years of marriage – may we continue to grow in Christ together.

Thank you to the four newlyweds who went through the course with me and helped me proofread the drafts – Marvin & Mabel, Roy & Sarah, Kinyip & Lydia, Ben & Celine. May you all truly reflect Christ and His Church.

Thanks to Simon Wong who began the premarital course in our church.

CHAPTER 1
THINGS CHANGE

George Bernard Shaw described it this way:

> *When two people are under the influence of the most violent, most insane, most delusive, and most transient of passions, they are required to swear that they will remain in that excited, abnormal, and exhausting condition continuously until death do them part.*

That's what the statistics tell us – when marriage starts, love disappears. So why bother getting married at all?

Marriage has been on the decline worldwide. In the US, it is estimated that 40-50% of all marriages end in divorce.[1] In the UK, cohabitation rates (living together without marriage) are increasing at alarming speed. It is the "fastest growing family type in the UK".[2]

Even in Singapore, although people are still getting married, the rate of divorce has been increasing steadily, especially among newly married couples.[3]

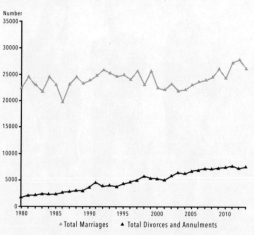

Number of marriages and divorces in Singapore (1980-2013)[4]

It seems that Mr Shaw was right all along – marriage is exhausting, and not many people can keep it up. Not surprisingly, this has created a deep sense of pessimism amongst many young adults considering long-term relationships.

So why do you want to get married again?

Oh, yes… The drive. We feel the drive, don't we? The physical and emotional need to be with another person. The desire to be close to someone, to share life with someone, to open up to someone, to have someone support you, listen to you, touch you, be with you… The drive. Yes, clearly, we were all made to be with someone else.

On one hand, we want to be with someone, but on the other hand, look at the stats, look at the relationships around you – even our parents and relatives – and we can't help but begin to doubt whether this thing called 'marriage' is possible, let alone worth it.

Let's throw another spanner into the works. In Asia, there is social pressure to marry. If you are not married, then there's something seriously 'wrong' with you. (Don't get me started on the pressure to have babies!)

Such a tension, isn't it? All these factors – the drive, the Asian pressure – coupled with a tremendous sense of doubt and fear of failure drive us to become more cynical.

So what is the answer?

Well… I guess it is to work on your selection process.

First, put all your energy into finding the right *one* for marriage. We create this 'checklist' to make sure that we filter out all the rotten apples and only look for the ones that are really juicy.

In fact, I dare say, the older we get, the more extensively we have dated, the more 'misses' we've had, the longer this list gets! We desire some form of safeguard that the person we marry will not disappoint.

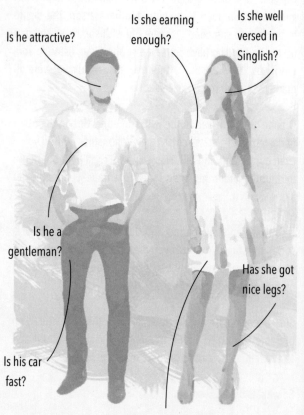

Second, once you are happy with the person from a distance, now we need to test out our relationship dynamics to see if we are really compatible physically, sexually, emotionally, spiritually, and financially.

Let's *test* each other out before we make that 'fateful choice' of *the one*! Let's date tons of people and see if they fit. Let's sleep with one another and see if it's hot. Oh, but it may only have been hot the first time. So let's keep doing it several more times just to make sure the passion doesn't fade.

Let's live with one another and see if we can tolerate each other for more than ten minutes. We've got to get an apartment, move in together, see if we can have synchronised laundry timings, eat the same food, and share the same taste in late night television.

Let's have children with one another to see if we can hack it. After all, nothing reveals compatibility more than having children, right?

Finally when all that is done – *then* let's get married! Because surely we've tested each other to death – and now we will never part!

But hang on – since we've done everything there is to be done, why get married?

Does it work? I'm not sure. Cohabitation 'divorce' statistics seem to be at least as high as marriage ones!

People go out of their way in the dating game and habits like cohabitation because they are always afraid that the person they have selected to marry is not going to be the 'right one'.

Even when we've found someone we really like, because of

all the horrible statistics, we are so hesitant to settle down with them in case they are not what they seem – in case they change! So we try to circumvent that by cohabiting with them for several years, so we can know everything about them and ensure that they won't change for the worse.

So many people get disappointed with marriage because so many people base their marriage choice on the fact that they have found someone who seems to meet all their current needs and demands, whether that refers to looks, income, social status, sexual experience, cultural traits, etc. You've found someone who 'fits' you at this present moment, and it seems that what they want in life is similar to what you want and so you get married.

We spend our whole lives looking for that perfect fit, and somehow we think that after such an exhaustive search, a ring on the finger will seal that person in that present state that you found him or her. The marriage ceremony becomes a sort of 'preservation' ceremony.

But the problem is that people *do* change.

People change.
Feelings change.
Emotions change.
Looks change.
Situations change.
Circumstances change.
Jobs change.
Shapes change.

That's why any marriage preparation course that uses a checklist – and makes that the definitive way of assuring you a happy future – is terrible. In fact it will set you up for an even greater disappointment. Imagine this scenario:

Jerald and Sharlene have been together for three years. Jerald had been dating another girl two years earlier, but that hadn't worked out because the young lady – while no doubt very attractive and successful – had no intention of having children in the near future. She didn't see herself as 'mother material'; so she said. Long story short, it ended.

Jerald then met Sharlene at a work function. She was just as pretty, yet after one conversation Jerald noticed that she was thinking of settling down and didn't want to have a full-time career in the future. Despite her stellar corporate performance, she liked the idea of having her own 'white picket fence' home, with 2.5 children and a dog. Jerald was immediately attracted – it seemed to fit in very well with his future plans.

So they dated for a year and his hopes were verified. She was exactly what he was looking for. And he was her ideal match as well, someone who would bring home the bacon but only to have it with Caesar salad, she said. They got along well, and decided that they should try moving in together. On their second anniversary he gave her a key to his city apartment and she gladly moved in.

Staying together was a challenge for sure. At first, he had to clear 20, then 30, then 70% of his stuff to make room for her vast collection of shoes. Then she insisted that he completely remodel his kitchen so that she could train up her cooking skills – she was going to be a domestic goddess after all! He didn't mind. He loved her. The sex was great. The household was well kept. She was pretty. They had much in common. Sure there was the occasional fight here and there, a few tears, a little bloodshed, but nothing major, of course.

In the third year they planned a wedding. They talked about a future life together and their plans were music to their ears – harmonious to the very detail. The wedding happened and it was grand! What a wonderful celebration! Their life together was just beginning!

Another two years passed, Sharlene resigned to have her first child. But there was a problem. There were complications in her womb towards the end of her third trimester. Many doctor's appointments were arranged. Surgery was scheduled. Sharlene made it; the child didn't. Later it was found out that future pregnancies would be ill advised and practically impossible. The 2.5 children dream was over.

They were devastated but made it through. Sharlene figured that since she wasn't going to be a mum (adoption never crossed their high-flying corporate Asian minds), she'd go back to work.

Hang on, thought Jerald. This wasn't the deal. That was not the kind of life they had planned for. He wanted a family home. He would work and she would take care of the children (maybe work part-time). Dogs, kids, gardens, BBQs in the sunshine, cycling in the park…. That kind of life.

Jerald began to get more and more upset with their circumstances. Sharlene thought he blamed her for the loss of their son. He didn't. But he kept thinking that this was not the life he wanted. His tone with her became harsher. Every small thing was her fault. Sharlene went into depression. "He hates me for killing our child," she said. "No, I don't," he said. And so their marriage went spiralling downward.

A year later, they divorced. The dream was over.

Things change. That is the only constant in this world. Everything *will* change. Nothing stands still.

What happens when a couple finds out they are unable to have children?
What happens when one day, this person gets old, and his/her looks fade?
What happens when they get fired from their high-paying job?
What happens when one gets cancer?
What happens when one day the sex doesn't seem that great anymore?
What happens when someone decides to change his/her religion?

There are no safety nets against the winds of change.

So if people are always going to change, how then does one get married? Is there any security we can base our marriage on if the one guarantee is that my partner will be different in five to ten years' time?

So what do we do?

Either we give up on marriage or we can approach marriage not by satisfying personal checklists, but by changing our mindsets.

What this book suggests is that if we change the way we think about marriage before entering marriage (even before we start dating), it could very well help us prepare for a married life that can handle the storms of change.

Mindset. Not safety net.

Be ready for change.

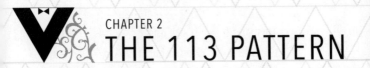

CHAPTER 2
THE 113 PATTERN

Let's get started on the mindset.

No apologies – we are talking about a Christian mindset. That means we need to change our minds about marriage based on who the Christian God, the Living God of the Bible, is. Marriage is something that reflects who the Christian God is.

Let us start off with this verse:

> But I want you to understand that the head of every man is Christ, the head of a wife is her husband, and the head of Christ is God. (1 Corinthians 11:3)

From this verse, straightaway you can see that the Scriptures make a couple of comparisons. Can you see them?

The writer compares the husband-and-wife relationship with that of Man and Christ, as well as Christ and God. Something like this:

Husband & Wife

Christ & Church

Father & Son

Here, the husband-and-wife relationship is really based on the much bigger and better relationship of Christ and the church. That is to say, the goal of the husband-and-wife relationship is to imitate the relationship between Christ and the church.

From 1 Corinthians 11:3, we can also see that Christ's relationship with the Church is itself based on the much bigger and better relationship of God (the Father) and Christ (the Son) – a relationship that has existed within the Godhead (Trinity) for all eternity!

Here's what one of my Bible teachers once said about comparing marriage to the relationship between the Father and the Son:

> *... the Father is the lover, the Son is the beloved....*
>
> *That turns out to be hugely significant, as the apostle Paul observes in 1 Corinthians 11:3: 'Now I want you to realise that the head of every man is Christ, and the head of the woman is man, and the head of Christ is God.'... And therein lies the very goodness of the gospel: as the Father is the lover and*

> *the Son the beloved, so Christ becomes the lover and the church the beloved....*
>
> *That dynamic is also to be replicated in marriages, husbands being the heads of their wives, loving them as Christ the Head loves his bride, the church. He is the lover, she is the beloved.... For eternity, the Father so loves the Son that he excites the Son's eternal love in response; Christ so loves the church that he excites our love in response; the husband so loves his wife that he excites her to love him back. Such is the spreading goodness that rolls out of the very being of this God.*[1]

God is three Persons. God is three Persons – Father, Son, and Spirit. God is three Persons – Father, Son, and Spirit loving one another. If you take a snapshot of God, what you would see is the Father loving the Son, and the Son responding in love to the Father – all this through the Spirit.

At His core, God is love. That means different Persons loving one another in a relationship.

So when He makes humanity, what does He make? When God wants to make a carbon copy of Himself, what comes out?

> *So God created man in his own image, in the image of God he created him; **male and female he created them**. (Genesis 1:27; emphasis mine)*

It's not just that Adam alone was in the image of God, but Adam and Eve together reflect who God really is. After all, just like Christ died for the church, so Adam was put into a 'death-like' sleep (Genesis 2:21), and out of his side came the flesh and bone to create Eve, the one who would be bone of his bone and flesh of his flesh. A companion suitable for Adam. Already in the Adam and Eve story we can see clearly the Christ and the church story. It is no surprise.

> *"Therefore a man shall leave his father and mother and hold fast to his wife, and the two shall become one flesh." This mystery is profound, and I am saying that it refers to Christ and the church. (Ephesians 5:31-32)*

We imitate or 'image' God not just on our own, but especially so when we form certain types of relationships with one another. The most dominant of these 'imaging' relationships is the one between husband and wife.

You see, all marriage has its roots and foundations in the divine nature – in the way God relates within the Trinity. And ultimately marriage becomes one of the greatest (or dare I say *the* greatest) ways of portraying who an invisible God is to the world.

John Piper, an American preacher, once put it this way:

> *Marriage is the doing of God, and ultimately, marriage is the display of God… It is*

> *designed by God to display His glory in a way that no other event or institution does.*[2]

Since God is three Persons in a loving relationship, then naturally humanity, being made in His image, would also consist of persons designed for relationship. Hence every person made in God's image has 'the drive', as we mentioned earlier – the deep desire to be connected with other persons in a profound way.

It is no wonder then that Jesus is often called our Bridegroom (John 3:29).

Marriage is something foundational to all humanity – two persons like the Father and the Son come together to love one another.

This is going to be the basis for all our marital advice. All we're going to do is to look at the different characteristics of the Father-Son (in the Spirit) relationship and see how that is reflected in the Christ-church (in the Spirit) relationship and filtered down to the husband-wife (in the Spirit) relationship.

So for the rest of this book, we are going to examine in detail a few aspects of the Father-Son relationship and see how it ultimately translates as our basis for the ideal husband-wife relationship.

Are you ready?

CHAPTER 3
RULES OF ENGAGEMENT

Let's start here.

How do the Father and the Son relate to each other? What are the dynamics of their relationship with one another?

Once we see that the same dynamics apply in the Christ-church relationship, we can then apply it to the husband-wife relationship.

As we read Scripture, we begin to realise that the Father relates to the Son by constantly affirming His love as a Father to Him. For example:

> ... and behold, a voice from heaven said, "This is my beloved Son, with whom I am well pleased." (Matthew 3:17)
>
> I will tell of the decree: The LORD said to me, "You are my Son; today I have begotten you." (Psalm 2:7)

> *Behold my servant, whom I uphold, my chosen, in whom my soul delights...*
> *(Isaiah 42:1a)*

The Father constantly affirms the Son as His *Chosen One* (that's what the word 'Christ' means!). And more than that – the Son whom He loves and delights in.

Verse by verse, we slowly begin to build a picture of a Father who has *chosen freely* to be a Father to His Son, to love His Son, and is committed to do everything to benefit the Son – so that the Son may be glorified.

We see more of this kind of relationship between Christ and the church. Just like the Son, the people of God (sons of God) are also referred to as His chosen ones:

> *O offspring of Israel his servant, sons of Jacob, his chosen ones! (1 Chronicles 16:13)*
>
> *Put on then, as God's chosen ones...*
> *(Colossians 3:12a)*

The ones whom He has chosen. The ones He decides to freely love. And not only are we chosen at the beginning, but more than that, He promises that once He has chosen us, He will always be with us, always put up with our nonsense, and stay by our side. He freely commits Himself to be eternally with those He has chosen:

> *... for he has said, "I will never leave you nor forsake you." (Hebrews 13:5b)*
>
> *And behold, I am with you always, to the end of the age. (Matthew 28:20b)*

So we get a picture of a God who chooses to engage with persons with a free love.

PLEASE SIGN ON THE DOTTED LINE

When we relate to one another, we tend to veer towards something called a contractual type of relationship.

In the 13th century, a Christian leader called Aelred of Rievaulx stated that humanity tends to form two types of friendships. One he termed "carnal", where two people are attracted to each other, but end up consuming one another. The second he termed "worldly", where each is "enkindled by the hope of gain" – two people come together to see what they can get out of each other, before finally discarding one another.[1]

In most relationships we want the other to benefit us. That's just human nature. No one wants to enter an unbeneficial relationship! And so when we see a person who can profit us, we are happy to form a relationship with them, but we will always set up a way of protecting ourselves from harm or from a 'bad investment' in our rules of engagement. That protectionist way of thinking leads us to draw up a contractual relationship.

In a contractual relationship, two parties make an agreement. When one party breaks that agreement… Let me put it this way: When one party *changes*, the agreement is broken.

That's how many people view marriage. They make a contract with each other: "I agree to be this person whom you see right here and now, and you agree to be that person whom I see right here and now. We know each other's current goals, dreams, plans, and ideals and we find them desirable and mutually beneficial. Henceforth we agree to relate to each other in a mutually beneficial and binding agreement from this day onward."

That's what most people *actually* say at marriage (okay, they don't say it with their lips but that's what they mean). They have a 'preservation ceremony' for a contract in which you will continue to look, act, and be exactly the same as how you are now. But once you change, then bye-bye… I didn't sign up for this! You betrayed me! I'm outta here! You broke your end of the deal!

Isn't that the case?

But in the relationship between the Father and the Son, the Father does not love the Son by contract. Can you imagine a father loving a son solely based on a contractual agreement? That family would fall apart in seconds! Children do all kinds of stupid things from the moment they are born. *Contracts are useless* at forming these kinds of relationships!

Why does a father love a son? I guess simply because he's his father and he has chosen to have a son, and now he loves the son with freely given love.

This freely given love is often called **covenant love** or unconditional love. It is a love where I love you because I love you. Or rather, because I have chosen to love you. No conditions supplied. There is no protection clause.

I think this type of love is best seen when we see God interact with the characters in the book of Genesis such as Abraham, Isaac, and Jacob.

When we look carefully, we see that these guys aren't really heroes. Actually, they have a lot of issues. Abraham begins to have doubts and marital problems really early on in his life.[2] Isaac is a bit… emo.[3] And Jacob… (sigh) Jacob is just Jacob. He's categorically hopeless until the final few days of his life!

Yet if we see how God deals with them, this is what happens:
1. God meets Patriarch.
2. God gives Patriarch a ridiculously wonderful promise!
3. Patriarch is very happy.
4. Promises don't materialise immediately.
5. Patriarch then realises this is going to be much harder and longer than he thought.
6. Patriarch does something foolish to either speed up the process or do things 'Frank Sinatra' style.[4]
7. God steps in and encourages foolish Patriarch, reiterating same promise.
8. Patriarch after ages and ages of struggling finally believes that God really does love Him.

The people God chooses are picked not because they are very loveable. In fact I suspect He sometimes selects the worst possible person just to prove a point! Then He promises to love them freely, which they initially get happy about, but then they eventually mess up because when things get difficult or when the waiting is prolonged they reveal that they don't really trust Him at all. Yet God never gives up on them and never rescinds His promise. That's the point of a promise – it has no contractual obligations on the recipient. Only on the Promiser!

This is what covenant love is all about. *It is choosing to love someone freely, and committing to love them no matter what happens from that point onwards.*

This is what defines a covenantal relationship. We love and commit to keep loving another person simply because that is what we have chosen to do. And it is free in the sense that this commitment to love is not bound by what the other person does in return!

This is the love that the Father lavishes on the Son through the Spirit. It is the love that Christ, who learns from the Father (see John 5:19), lavishes upon the church through the Spirit. And it is the love that husbands are called to lavish upon their wives, through the Spirit.

THE PROMISE

In order to inaugurate a covenant or unconditional love relationship between two persons, we need to have a declaration of love to the other person. In the Scriptures, such declarations of Christ to His church come in the form of promises or vows. They come in the form of the "I will" statements:

> … *I will be with you and will bless you…*
> *(Genesis 26:3)*
>
> … *I will be with you. I will not leave you or forsake you. (Joshua 1:5)*
>
> … *this is the covenant that I will make with the house of Israel after those days, declares the LORD: I will put my law within them, and I will write it on their hearts. And I will be their God, and they shall be my people. (Jeremiah 31:33)*
>
> … *I will be a Father to you, and you shall be sons and daughters to me, says the Lord Almighty. (2 Corinthians 6:18)*
>
> … *I will be merciful toward their iniquities, and I will remember their sins no more. (Hebrews 8:12)*

So many "I will" promises given by God to His people – and not on the basis of anything they have done or deserved, but on the basis of God's free choice of love.

Marriage is essentially a promise that initiates covenant love between two persons: I promise to love you... Without any condition.

In the traditional Christian wedding vow, this is what each person is asked:

> *Soon-to-be-husband, will you have this lady as your wedded wife, to live together according to God's Word in the holy institution of matrimony? Will you love her, comfort her, honour and keep her, in all circumstances; and, forsaking all others, keep yourself only for her, so long as you both shall live?*

> *Soon-to-be-wife, will you have this gentleman as your wedded husband, to live together according to God's Word in the holy institution of matrimony? Will you love him, serve him, honour and submit to him in the Lord, in all circumstances; and, forsaking all others, keep yourself only for him, so long as you both shall live?*

You are asked to make your own "I will" statement to one another. And after that is done, to state that love for one another in the form of a vow or a promise:

> *I, soon-to-be-husband, take you, lady, as my wedded wife, to have and to hold, from this day forward, for better for worse, for richer for poorer, in sickness and in health, to love, to lead and to cherish, till death do us part, according to God's Word; and for this I give you my solemn pledge.*

> *I, soon-to-be-wife, take you, gentleman, as my wedded husband, to have and to hold, from this day forward, for better for worse, for richer for poorer, in sickness and in health, to love, to cherish and to submit in the Lord, till death do us part, according to God's Word; and for this I give you my solemn pledge.*

Just in case you didn't realise what unconditional means, it means: For better or for worse, for richer or for poorer, in sickness and in health, in all circumstances, no matter what happens to you or to me, I choose to freely love you till death.

It is how God loves His Son. It is how Christ loves the church. It is how a husband is supposed to love his wife.

In a Christian marriage, the marriage is not about signing legal documents, buying a house, or even turning up very nicely dressed in a church. The primary thing about the Christian marriage is the promise we say to one another, which reflects the promises that Christ made to us. And it begins a relationship between two persons that would reflect the eternal relationship between the Father and the Son.

A marriage is a promise-bound relationship. It is begun by the word of the promise.

If I dare say so, the vow *is* the marriage. The vow is the marriage because it is the one that sets up the fact that from this day forward, you will now begin to interact with one another according to new rules of engagement. You have freely promised to love one another, and you have sealed it not with a kiss or a ring, but with a vow. The ring and the kiss are simply signs of such powerful promise words.

A good friend of mine once wrote:

> *"What is a marriage? Covenant union. God's covenant: "I will be your God, you will be my people." Unconditional love: "I love you because I love you." Conditionality is the killer!*[5]

Marriage at its core involves words spoken over each other that speak of this covenant, this unconditional love. These words are embodied in the traditional wedding vow. We make a free promise to love one another unconditionally – *even if you change*, I have once and for all freely promised to love you!

Here's John Piper again:

> *Staying married, therefore, is not mainly about staying in love. It is about keeping covenant. "Till death do us part" or "As long as we both shall live" is a sacred covenant promise – the same kind Jesus made with his bride when he died for her.*[6]

Are you ready to get married?

At this moment you may be asking yourself: How can I make such a crazy promise? To love someone without any conditions? Who could do such a thing?

I once had a conversation with a good friend:

> FRIEND: I don't think I'm ready to get married yet.
> ME: Why not?
> FRIEND: I can't say that kind of vow. I don't know

> if I'll be able to live it out. For example, what happens when we have our second child (he hadn't even gotten married or had his first yet) and the child is disabled, so much so that we have to use what we saved for the first child's university education to pay for the second child's medical bills and that causes the first child to resent us, which makes my wife very unhappy, and causes irreconcilable marital issues that may end up in divorce? What then?
>
> ME: ???

Can you feel his sentiment? *So many possibilities!* Hundreds of permutations. How could I make such a promise if I don't even know what could happen?

How would you answer such a question?

Well, I have two answers to that question.

Answer 1
We can make this promise if we know and have experienced such a promise that has been made to us.

God never expected us to be able to make such claims on our own accord. This is what He told us: "We love because he first loved us" (1 John 4:19).

This is not some arbitrary or over-sentimental statement. It is a profound and experiential truth. We can only love if we have been loved.

Marriage exposes one thing: Do you know the covenant love of God? Because if you do, then you are able to make a similar promise to another.

If you have seen God stick with you in difficult times, you can stick with your spouse. If you have seen God's faithfulness to you when you betrayed Him, you can be faithful when your spouse betrays you. If you have seen God comfort, encourage, strengthen, and support you when you felt like giving up… you can comfort, encourage, strengthen, and support your spouse when he or she is about to give up.

Marriage is one of the truest tests of an experienced relationship with God. Hence it is not surprising that marriage becomes one of the primary analogies of the gospel in Scripture, and it is one of the chief ways that the world will see an invisible God:

> *What is a marriage? Gospel presentation. One man and one woman bound together the way Christ is united to His church. It is a gospel proclamation: "All that I am I give to you, all that I have I share with you." Christ says that to you. Do you know this to be true? Now you say it to each other… and the world looks on and sees the gospel. Your marriage preaches – for good or ill! But you can't stop it preaching.*[7]

> *Therefore, what makes divorce and remarriage so horrific in God's eyes is not merely that it involves covenant breaking to the spouse, but that it involves misrepresenting Christ and His covenant… Marriage is not mainly about being or staying in love. It's mainly about telling the truth with our lives. It's about portraying something true about Jesus Christ and the way He relates to His people. It is about showing in real life the glory of the gospel.*[8]

It is when we know such a powerful love for us that we can even hope to make such a crazy promise to another person, knowing that they will change, knowing that they will fail us, knowing that they are not perfect.

Answer 2
The vow itself has power to change us.

Yes, the more we know God's covenant love, the more we can make the free promise to perpetually love someone else. But saying the vow also has the power to change our actions.

What do I mean?

Let's imagine…

You marry. We give you a house. And now you have to stay in this house with your new spouse without ever leaving the house. You have all the resources that you need in the house but you are not supposed to leave. There is only one way in and out of this house – and it's through the front door. The door is wide open.

Now after a while, it is inevitable that you will quarrel with your spouse. Surely there will be something about the way this person lives or interacts with you that will greatly annoy you, and you have an argument. You begin to fight, words are exchanged, voices are raised, tempers flare up. The issue seems unresolvable. No one is listening to each other, you're about ready to throw things at the other person – and you see the wide open door. That's the solution – run! So you grab your stuff and bolt out of the door. The argument is never resolved, and you may or may not return.

That's the first scenario. Now imagine again…

Exactly the same situation, same house, same spouse. But this time the front door is locked. It was completely sealed as soon as the two of you entered. You are not supposed to leave as well.

Again, after a while, a quarrel arises. Temperatures rise. The both of you get all flustered. You threaten to rearrange the furniture (and perhaps your spouse's face). You try to make a run for it – but oh, wait… The door is locked. So now what do you do? What can you do?

After a few days of shouting, a cold war begins. As long as the argument exists, both your lives are miserable. The household is a disaster.

Weeks pass, and you get seriously fed up of sleeping on the floor, eating what's left in the last remaining cereal box, the laundry pile has reached the ceiling, the toilet has gotten clogged and it's beginning to reek. What can you do?

You look at your spouse… Breathe a heavy sigh and say, "I'm sorry. Shall we talk it out?"

Your spouse looks incredulously back at you and is about to shout but then says, "Sigh… Me too. What was the fight about anyway?"

Neither of you remember but you get to cleaning up the house and sorting out the relationship, vowing never to do that again (at least until tomorrow).

What made the difference?

The locked door.

I once watched a short film about a medical doctor.[v] It's a true story, written as a micro-documentary:

> He was looking at this photo of himself on holiday with his wife and two children. He said it was the 'happiest moment of his life'. They had an awesome family.
>
> However, a few years later, his wife was diagnosed with a complicated brain tumour, and ended up in a coma for 5½ years.
>
> His daughter came up to him one night and asked, "Daddy, why does it have to be our mummy?" He held her close and they both cried all night.
>
> Yet each day, after work, he would head to the hospital to read to his wife, tell her about his day, and play her some music before he heads home to be with the children. All this even as she just lies there, motionless, in that comatose state.

Initially he confessed that his love for his wife was a romantic love, but it later evolved and progressed into something much more concrete – 'a love that required work'. A love that as he said, "Became the outworking of a vow."

As the video ended, we hear the doctor restating those wonderful marriage vows to his wife, and we see a cross in the background.

That's a true story. That's how a vow works.

A vow removes the open door of divorce from your mind. You need to mentally lock the door in your marriage. When you are in you are *all in*. It is a sealed relationship. There is no way out.

When you can do this in your heart and your head, that is when you will see the power of the vow.

> *This is what the marriage vows are for… The vows exist because sin is real. Sure, we may not know what sins will become real in our relationships, putting stress on the covenant, but the vows exist because sin does.*[10]

As long as the vow is a theoretical one, meaning if it's just talk, it has no power. The power of the vow is based on the convictions of the Promiser. If you mean it when you say it, delete the word 'divorce' from your vocabulary (you may want to comfort yourself by saying that murder is a possibility – but divorce is definitely not![11]). Then when things go wrong, when things *change*, you will see how powerful a vow really is.

It is the vow that has the power to change you.

> *A troubled couple says "We don't love each other anymore." The solution: "Love each other then!" "Don't love her because she's beautiful, love her to make her beautiful." Unconditional love has power to cleanse and rename. In the context of unconditional love, there is the power to reshape our identity."*[12]

If you don't make a vow, then nothing can ever combat change or difficulty. If you do make that vow, put all the seriousness you can muster to heave that door of marriage, seal it shut, and weld it tight. Now you can watch what happens. You will have first row seats to witness the power of covenant love.

But only if you lock the door.

JUST SAY IT
In marriage we have no idea what is going to happen.

People change. You will be amazed by how much your spouse will annoy or upset you, and this annoyance at a changing person or even circumstances can become the root of all marital issues – leading to long-term quarrels, emotional distance, or even divorce.

Yet God has given us the very tool for growing lifelong relationships. It's called a promise.

A minister (whose name I didn't manage to catch) once said at a wedding: "I'm amazed at how much time, energy, and effort goes into planning the most intricate details at each wedding but how little time is spent meditating on the vow."

How true that is. We don't just say this vow once, when the marriage begins. The real trick is to say it – that promise of freely chosen love – again, and again, and again to each other.

The Scriptures have another word for this covenant or unconditional love. Sometimes it is called a "steadfast love" (Lamentations 3:22). And do you know how that steadfast love is defined? It is a love that is "new every morning" (Lamentations 3:23). That is to say that each morning God loves us with a 'fresh love'. He determines Himself to say "I love you" again, and again, and again.

Regardless of what happened yesterday – a fight, a quarrel, a cold shoulder, a forgotten birthday, a lousy day at work, financial problems, and children issues. The next morning, all that is cast aside. It's a new day and a renewed love! It's new every morning! Just like you need freshly brewed coffee to start the day, you need freshly brewed love, too!

That is what we need to train ourselves to do. You don't just say your vow once at the altar. You need to renew that vow every single day, with a fresh "I love you" to your spouse!

Just say the vow, and keep saying it!

JESUS' VOW

Let me end this chapter with this quote:

> *When we stand at the altars making our vows, we really don't think the bad will be that bad. We expect sin but not that kind. But our holy bridegroom Jesus Christ makes his vow knowing full well what he's forgiving. He knows us inside and out. He knows what we're guilty of and what we will be guilty of. He knows just how awful it's going to get.*
>
> *If Jesus were keeping a list of our wrongs, none of us would stand a chance. At any*

> *second of any second of any day, even on our best days, Jesus could have the legal grounds to say, "Enough of this. I can't do it anymore. You've violated my love for the last time." The truth is, you've never met a wronged spouse like Jesus. You've never met a disrespected spouse like Jesus. You've never met a spouse who more than carried their weight like Jesus. He's carrying the entire relationship on his back. This thing is totally one-sided.*
>
> *And yet: He loves. And he gives. And he serves. And he approves. And he washes. And he delights. And he romances. And he doesn't just tolerate us; he lavishes his affection on us. He justifies and sanctifies and glorifies…*
>
> *Be still, our beating hearts. Here's a groom worth swooning over.*[13]

If you want a good Christian marriage, we need to think about the vow. Not just the vow *you* are going to make, but more than that – think about the vow that *God* has made in Christ to you. A vow that transcends all annoyance, goes beyond all upsetting, and is out of a free love that has committed itself to you by His Spirit.

Don't be afraid of the vow. Think deeply about the vow. Delight in the vow.

MARITAL EXERCISE 1
LOCKING THE DOOR

Before you actually get married, do a little mental exercise:

Face each other and close your eyes.

Imagine that you are going into a small room with your future spouse. Go into the room with him/her and slowly close that door. Take out a key, lock that door. Throw away the key.

Now open your eyes and say to each other:

> "We are going to be bound for life. When we say our vows we are locking that door.
>
> The word 'divorce' will never leave our lips.
>
> For better or for worse, we are in this room together.
>
> Through fights and through fears, we will never leave each other.
>
> I will be with you always.
>
> Just like God has always been with me."

MARITAL EXERCISE 2
FRESHLY BREWED LOVE

Each day make a commitment to say "I choose to love you freely" to your spouse. Say it in the morning, every morning. Fix a time to say it. Say to one another. Look into each other's eyes while saying it.

Make that statement fresh each day, like your morning coffee. "I love you."

Say it especially when you've had quarrels the night before. Say it, and seal it with a kiss!

You can start even before you actually get married, but make sure the wedding has already been planned – if it doesn't work out, it will be very disappointing, and will lower the 'power of the promise' in your mind.

CHAPTER 4
WHEN TWO BECOME ONE (I)

> *Therefore a man shall leave his father and mother and hold fast to his wife, and the two shall become one flesh. (Ephesians 5:31)*

Two becoming one. That pretty much sums up the *goal* of marriage.

Two persons come together to become one. What does that mean?

BACK TO THE 113 PATTERN
Remember that we are basing our marriage mindset wholly on the relationship that the Father has with the Son through the Spirit. So we know that the husband and wife become one, just like the Father and the Son are one: "I and the Father are one" (John 10:30).

Or more specifically: "… just as you, Father, are in me, and I in you…" (John 17:21).

For two persons to be one, it means they have to be 'in' each other. It essentially means for two persons to remain as two persons but to become so intertwined, to 'inter-penetrate' each other so deeply, that all their desires, goals, hopes, dreams, and even likes and dislikes become complementary.

It means getting to a place where both persons essentially resonate with one another. Where each fills each other's sweet spot. Lock and key, two broken hearts coming together – you've heard all the cheesy phrases. But that's what it's all about. For two people to come so close to one another that, in Jerry Maguire's[1] words, "You complete me". That sums up our drive for relationships.

You see, the Father and the Son have always been each other's completers. They love each other and have grown so close to one another that they have no need for anyone else![2]

That is the goal for Christ and the church. That is perhaps the deepest thing that Christ desires for His church:

> ... that they may all be one, just as you, Father, are in me, and I in you, that they also may be in us... that they may be one even as we are one, I in them and you in me, that they may become perfectly one... (John 17:21-23)

That is His deep desire for all believers.

In mimicking the Father and the Son, and Christ and the church, this same oneness applies as the goal for husband and wife.

In the story of Adam and Eve, Eve was made to 'complete' Adam. She was taken from Adam's side while he underwent a near-death experience, and then brought back to his side to complete him. Adam was not good alone.

So it is with Christ and the church. So it *should be* with every husband and wife.

TWO PORCUPINES

The trick here is to see that this compatibility does not happen from the outset. In the gospel story of Christ and His church, Christ is the perfect bridegroom, while the church is often described as this terrible adulterous wife (see the book of Hosea). They most certainly form an unlikely pair!

Oneness does not happen at the start of marriage. Oneness is the *goal* of marriage! Two completely different persons say a covenant vow in order that they may *become* one!

Marriage in past eras was never based on compatibility – well, at least not as much as in modern dating today. In the past it was all about arranged marriage. Sure, you would know a few things about the other person, usually via parents talking to other parents, but it was hardly anything, really! All you knew was that one day you were living your own single life, and the next day you were in bed with this stranger who suddenly becomes your whole world. I'm sure many people would have had a 'Jacob-Leah' moment![3]

So how would it work?

It did – because people were perhaps more 'programmed' (culturally and socially) to understand that a marriage is about two persons resolving differences, rather than having a pre-arranged compatibility study!

I have at least two sets of friends (besides my wife and I) who come from very different backgrounds. Different countries, different races, different political systems, different educational upbringing, different parental styles, different cultural outlooks, and yet they still got married. At that point, they only knew one or two things about each other – in most cases they shared a strong Christian faith – and that seemed to be enough.

All these couples have thriving marriages today, with great families, despite the fact that they knew each other just a few months before their wedding ceremonies.

Now how is that possible?

It is possible because they have a different mindset to marriage. They are big Spice Girls fans... They know it's about two becoming one.[4]

Even when two people think they are so similar to one another before they come together at marriage, how often do we find that when all the clothes are off, when we have the 'real me' and the 'real you' standing before one another, we are simply not who we expected. There is only the *illusion* of similarity. But in reality we are all strangers:

> *We never know whom we marry; we just think we do... the primary problem is... learning to love and care for the stranger to whom you find yourself married.*[5]

What do you expect? Everyone is a sinner, thus everyone is *incompatible* by definition!

> *Some people... do not see marriage as two flawed people coming together to create a space of stability, love and consolation... The assumption is that there is someone*

> *just right for us to marry and that if we look closely enough we will find the right person… It fails to appreciate the fact that we always marry the wrong person…*[6]

Ever heard the story of two porcupines?[7]

> *Once upon a time there were two porcupines. Winter came and it began to get very cold. One porcupine looked and saw that the other porcupine suddenly became very attractive. He was warm and she imagined that they would be real cosy if she could just snuggle up to him. So they touched snouts and admired one another's glossy spines. And finally he-porcupine said to she-porcupine: "I think you and I should be together."*
>
> *She agreed and moved into his humble abode after a little porcupine dance, which sealed the mating ceremony. That night she-porc finally got what she was waiting for – she snuggled up to he-porc and oh, yes, it was very warm! It was everything she ever dreamed of… Until "Ouch!" he said, "Ouch, ouch! Ouch!"*

> *She wondered what was going on… And then, "Ouch!" she cried too.*
>
> *They saw that their spines were too close and now they were poking one another repeatedly. No matter which way they twisted and turned, the spines kept digging in their exposed soft bellies.*
>
> *Suddenly she-porc saw he-porc in a different light. She realised she had 'snow-goggles' on when she first saw him. He was not the warm fluffy dream-bod she always wanted, but a cold prickly so-and-so. Oh, how she had been betrayed!*
>
> *She untangled herself from his prickles, packed her acorns, and shuffled out the hole of their little burrow, never to be seen again.*

Wonder if that often happens in marriages?

Before we get married, we suss each other out and we think we've worked out all the bugs. But once we get married, suddenly there is a stranger before us, and we think we've made a mistake.

If you think that way, you haven't changed your mindset about marriage. Thing is, you always marry the wrong person. You always marry a stranger.

That is the story of Christ and the church: The wonderful Bridegroom marries the terrible harlot.

The goal of marriage is to become one. Saying the vow and locking the door is the first step. If the door is open, then oneness is impossible. But after we lock the door, we have to *work* to become one.

BECOMING ONE

Some of my friends who got married added this beautiful ritual to their marriage ceremony. The husband and wife would each light a candle, and this would symbolise their individual lives. Then they would bring their candle to a bigger different-coloured candle in the middle of the church, and each of them would simultaneously use their flames to light the bigger candle. After the bigger candle was lit, they would each blow out their own candle flames. Two became one.

It is a powerful analogy of two people living two separate lives now committing to live only one life from this moment on. As you can easily visualise, it involves some 'dying to self'. It is all too easy for marriage partners to simply be co-workers on parallel paths rather than companions on a journey together.

What do I mean? I mean that often people think that marriage involves two persons whose lives just happen to be compatible 'by chance'. That is to say, at the moment of marriage, your work schedules fit, your career ambitions fit, your family planning seems to be in agreement, etc. You think that your lives are compatible – without you having to make any effort whatsoever!

The real problem is that paths are never compatible. No two people's lifelines are ever truly parallel! Even if it seems that they are at marriage, they are always just so slightly at an angle. And if no effort is made to converge the paths, then the two will inevitably drift away.

You see this all too often in young couples. They get married and are all happy and blissful, and immediately after the short honeymoon, they go back to living their lives in exactly the same way they did as before they were married. Same careers, same habits, same timetables, same friends… Okay, maybe now they are sharing one bed. But essentially they are two persons with two lives who are merely sleeping together (or at least we hope they are sleeping together after marriage – these days even sex within marriage seems to be asking for too much from one another!).

This pattern of life seems to be okay for a while, and if you ask them, they don't see any problems. They all seem to be happily married, like Rob and Sue:

> Rob and Sue had claimed that they were deeply in love. They had been together for about five years before deciding it was time to get married.
>
> Everyone thought it was a good idea. After all, they were so well matched – they shared

the same life stage, goals, dreams, and faith. It didn't seem like they had any problems or major arguments at all. Everything just 'fit'. So marry they did!

Then they got on with their lives, working in their different careers.

One day, Sue had to take a business trip. She had to go to another country for more than a month to work on an intensive corporate deal, together with a small team from her firm. Rob didn't mind – he thought it had good career prospects (which it did).

Sue soon left together with two other ladies and two other men from her company. They all lived in the same service apartment while working more than 15 hours a day to complete the project.

Sue worked closely with one guy in particular, Max, for her portion of the assignment. Every day they talked together, worked together in close quarters, and solved problems together. They worked hard; they were a great team. Every night, they'd have late dinners together, still talking about the project, but often straying into talking about life and possibilities in general.

Week after week passed, and they worked so much in sync that they could do work without conferring with the other. They were even finishing each other's sentences.

The moment came to give the final presentation. The whole team agreed that Sue and Max would be most suitable to do it. It was a resounding success, and the deal went through! The whole team was exuberant – they went out for a splendid meal and stayed up drinking all night.

The next morning, Sue woke up and found herself in Max's bed. "Oh no!" she thought, "This is terrible, what have I done?"

And yet, she found herself not jumping out of the bed. Looking at Max sleeping, a part of her wanted to stay.

How did that happen?

Couples who often don't see any obvious problems in their relationships 'suddenly' have affairs. What was the problem? Were they not really committed to one another when they said the vows? Was it just the overseas romance or the ecstasy of winning a corporate contract or maybe even the alcohol?

No. Things like that don't just happen. Things like that expose the reality that someone's heart is not 'filled'. The relationship with their spouse did not complete them in a sufficient way such that they were protected from the intrusions of another person. They never ended up embarking on the 'oneness' journey. They were simply two people, living two lives, who happened to have a ring on their fingers.

Rob and Sue were married because they thought they lived compatible lives, but they put no work into becoming one. Sue and Max worked very hard together – and ended up becoming more 'one' than they expected!

That's how it works: When two people work to become one, they start to 'fill each other up'. They satisfy one another like water to a thirsty throat. The more they fill each other, the more they find completeness in one another, and the less likely someone else can sneak into their soul.

This sneaking never happens overnight! It happens in small doses – a look here, a conversation there, a late night tonight, a meal tomorrow. We're letting another person fill us up instead of our spouse. We need to redirect all those small actions and refocus them on our spouse, so that they will fill us up instead. Anyone can fill our souls if we let them.

That's also how Jesus would describe his relationship with the church, like a bridegroom filling up a thirsty bride's soul (think of the woman at the well in John 4). He is supposed to be the one who satisfies all our needs, desires, and aspirations, and fills the void that the woman's five husbands never did. Jesus is the true spouse who can satisfy, while our spouses are supposed to mimic that satisfaction to a lesser extent. At least to the extent that our hearts are full enough to resist the temptation of another colleague working in close proximity!

But even with Jesus, it is not so easy to become one to the point of satisfying and resonating with each other. It takes time and effort.[8] Likewise, if you are going to be one with your spouse, you need to put in the work!

SIX MAJOR ISSUES

There are so many things that need to be worked out in a marriage, and you need to discuss them. You cannot simply live lives on parallel tracks; neither can you assume that things will just 'somehow happen'. You need to discuss these issues in detail and decide how things are going to happen.

Let me give you a list of some of the things that need to be worked on:

1. Careers
- ▼ What are your career plans for the next five to ten years?
- ▼ Do your work plans tie in with each other?
- ▼ How is your current work schedule? Do you have enough time to spend with one another?

2. Finances
- ▼ How are you going to settle the bills in your family? Are you going to have a joint account?
- ▼ What are your financial priorities?
- ▼ Do you have outstanding debts or loans (even unofficial ones with friends and family members) that need to be repaid?

3. Children
- ▼ Will you have children? When? How many?
- ▼ Will one of you stop work? For how long?

Note: When you have children you'll need another round of these discussions again!

4. In-Laws
- ▼ How will you spend time with your parents and your spouse's parents?
- ▼ What happens if your parents or in-laws have different views from your spouse?
- ▼ Are you going to set aside money on a regular basis for your in-laws or relatives?

5. Friends
- ▼ Do you want to keep your social circles separate (i.e. my friends are my friends)?
- ▼ How will you manage your time between your spouse and your friends?

▼ Are you comfortable if your spouse has many friends of the opposite sex?

6. Spiritual Life
▼ How big of a deal is church to the two of you? Will you be serving together?
▼ What about Christian fellowship – is it a priority? In what way?
▼ How will you help each other's spiritual maturity?

These questions are just the tip of the iceberg, but hopefully they get you thinking about the major issues that will arise in marriage.

Initially, of course, you will have differences. And even if you think you don't, you will soon find out you do! But the process of marriage is to work out these differences slowly and patiently with one another, not to dismiss the differences.

If you've worked out these issues here and now, trust me, new issues will come up. And once again, people *change*, so you will find yourselves having to work out the very issue that you thought had been put to bed!

You need to keep working at it throughout married life. In fact, you need to set a pattern of working things through constantly with your spouse.

CHAPTER 5
WHEN TWO BECOME ONE (II)

A NEW CENTRE

Having regular open communication and discussion about issues is not enough. There is a fundamental change in thinking that must happen for any future discussions to be fruitful.

Spouses need to be able to *trust each other* when working out issues in this new family. If there is no trust, and then no matter how rationally or well thought out the issue is and no matter how reasonable you try to be – you will still be unable to come to a resolution. No trust, no decisions. No trust, no walking together!

Trust does not come naturally. It needs to be earned. I dare say that working on this 'trust bank' is going to be the *prime work* in the early years (if not always!) of marriage.

If you don't trust one another, then when you have a different style of doing things, or the two of you seem to be going in different career directions, it's going to be hard to reconcile anything!

This works in the relationship between Christ and the church, too. Christ often commands us to do many things. But we don't listen.

Why not?

Because we don't trust Him. We don't have faith in Him. With faith comes obedience.[1] The more we trust Him, the more we listen to Him, the more we realise that everything He commanded us to do was for our own good. And the more we have experienced this goodness, the more we trust Him and listen to Him again. It's an upward spiral!

The negative is also true. The more we don't trust, the more we don't listen, and the more we blame Him (or others) for our misfortune. We need to earn each other's trust. As sinful creatures we are inherently untrusting. To earn each other's trust, you need to go all in!

When companies have discussions about their plans and the future, many people can have differing opinions. It's all too easy to say something and then cut and run once the ship is sinking. But if you want opinions that are valuable, first you have to make sure there is a certain element of loyalty and trust. If the people around that table have put their entire life savings into this company, you can be sure there's some weight to what they say! If they are simply a hired hand or a part-time employee, or some consultant, it's still good to listen to their experience, but in the end, this is not their life.

In a *new* marriage, the best way to earn each other's trust is to show each other that you are *all in*. That is to say, this relationship ought to take priority over any relationship or activity in your previously single life.[2]

The first year of your marriage is crucial for this:

> *When a man is newly married, he shall not go out with the army or be liable for any other public duty. He shall be free at home one year to be happy with his wife whom he has taken. (Deuteronomy 24:5)*

Even old Moses knew that, and put in a law that would ensure husbands and wives spend the very first year of marriage taking the time and energy to grow together – he banned the man from national service during that time![3]

As an individual you had your own priorities. It may have been your family, job, hobbies, friends, ambitions, etc. But that was you, as just you. Your life would have been centred on one of these things. In other words, the basis of your decision making would have been one of these things. That's how you know what is at the centre.

When you are married, you have to re-centre. Your decision making must now revolve around your spouse. Or more precisely, in decision making, the relationship you have with your spouse is the number one priority.[4] However, re-centring is enormously difficult to do!

If, for so many years, you made all your decisions to please your parents, it isn't going to change automatically such that you now make all your decisions to please your spouse. If, for so many years, your number one priority was your career path, one night of passion with your wife (no matter how amazing) isn't suddenly going to make her your new ambition!

You need to put whatever you can in place to tell yourself that you have a new centre now.

That Law of Moses is a great commandment. Immediately after you are married, spend the first year of marital life just doing things with your spouse. Never mind how long you were attached as boyfriend and girlfriend. This is something new, something different.

In the first year of marriage you need to *earn* each other's trust by *proving* to one another that you are all in. What can you do to do this?

First, isolate the old things that used to define you. It could be:

Parents (family)

Career (ambitions)

Hobbies
(personal life)

Friends
(social life)

Ministry
(church life)

Which one of these things defines you? What gives you the biggest sense of identity other than being a beloved child of God?

All these things must now come secondary to your marriage if you want to achieve oneness. You need to demonstrate to your spouse that they truly are secondary. That is not to say that you simply chuck them away, but you need to prove to one another that they are not as important as the other person. The more you do this in the early stage of marriage, the better!

In Scripture this is also known as leaving and cleaving.[5] Cutting off an old way of life to embark on another way of life. How do you do this? I can only give some suggestions.

Parents

This is the *number one* argument-generating issue in terms of Asian marriages!

▼ Try and find your own living space if you can afford it. If not, and you have to live with your relatives, do whatever you can to have some personal space for just the two of you. Live by a different set of rules than your parents or in-laws in that same house. Define your own house rules from the start. Identify things that you liked and disliked about the way your parents ran their household. Share with one another things that you want to keep and discard in your own household.

▼ Fix a limit to the amount of time spent at your parents' or in-laws'. Don't simply let them dictate that you must come and have dinner with one of them every night of the week. Respect them, but don't give in to emotional blackmail. Your spouse is the number one priority – make sure there is time for him/her!

My senior pastor once wrote:

> *When a man marries, he and his wife establish a new umbrella of authority. From then on, they are responsible for themselves and in time to come, for their children as well… In marriage the husband-wife relationship becomes the priority human relationship. Before marriage, his most important relationship is with his parents. In marriage, it is with his wife… The principle is a difficult one to accept. It runs against the grain of our (oriental) culture.*[6]

There are way too many stories of young couples with *massive* in-law problems because they don't know how to break away from that old umbrella.

Frank's parents expected them at their house for dinner every night. Germaine's parents happened to be in another country, so that meant that it wasn't an issue to visit them, except on holidays.

This initially seemed like a good deal for the young couple, since they were both busy working professionals, and having someone cook dinner for them every night was a bonus!

They soon had children, and Frank and Germaine now had to make more fundamental decisions on how to raise them. Not surprisingly, Frank's mother had a lot of 'advice' to give, which began to annoy Germaine greatly.

Germaine also wanted to do some of her own cooking for her children and work on her own style of parenting, so that meant spending fewer nights over at her in-laws' place. The in-laws were not pleased and started to visit often – unannounced! And when they couldn't visit, they would call repeatedly!

Germaine was going out of her mind. Frank, like most Asian men, thought that he shouldn't do anything because that wouldn't be 'filial' to his parents. Yet Germaine was desperately hoping he would stand up to his mother and tell her to give them some space.

> This ended up causing tremendous tension in their own marriage, and of course, spilled over to the whole household.

Does this story sound familiar to you? It happens in so many Asian families, when mothers don't let their sons 'go' to have some space with their wives. If only Frank and Germaine had set the boundaries up as soon as their marriage began, perhaps this wouldn't have been such a problem.

Men, you need to be very clear about this, especially with your own parents! In the end you need to choose only one voice to listen to. Is it going to be your wife's or your mother's? Whose voice will have the final say? You can't pretend that both are possible. You need to make up in your mind that your spouse has a higher priority than your parents.

For example, your parents ask you to give 20% of your income to them, but your spouse says that you need the money. After extensive negotiation, your parents still don't budge and your spouse is only willing to go up to 5%. What will you do then? You need to choose! You need to listen to one over the other. Most certainly you will cause an upset in one relationship by those choices. But you are under a different 'umbrella' now, and your immediate nuclear family is priority. Build the trust with your spouse.

Yes, it may be very offensive to your parents in the beginning. It will even sound like you hate them, even though you clearly don't.[7] It may sound very callous and harsh at the start, but everyone will appreciate it in the end – especially your wife.

You need to trust that building up your spousal relationship and giving it priority over your parents and in-laws is the best thing to do to re-align these deeply emotional relationships in their new and proper order. I think you will be pleasantly surprised at what will happen if you can do this right.

Career

▼ Go for a honeymoon together immediately after marriage (don't just go back to work the next day, for heaven's sake). I find this is really important to set the tone – everything *drops* for marriage! Demonstrate to each other that your spouse is more important than your careers.

▼ In the first year, try to cut down on business trips. Use the time to build up the family, not the career. I know that's really hard, but which one takes priority? Is career to feed family? Or is family to build career? Decide what the chief priority is and invest heavily in that one. New relationships require a heavy initial capital set-up.

▼ Once, you may have wanted to take that overseas assignment for three years. Rearrange it to become short business trips and spend those three years building your family.

▼ Once, you may have desired to be a partner of your law firm. Perhaps the work hours required to do so may be very upsetting to your spouse. Consider a lower target or a longer career path.

▼ You need to prove to your spouse that your career comes second to him/her. And more than that, that your career is only to benefit your family. This will be a very hard thing to get your head around, especially for workaholics.

Friends

There was once a young couple that wanted to get married. They were in love, and thought themselves highly compatible. Their parents approved and they got engaged.

However they came from very different social circles. The guy was more quiet and aloof, and had a few good friends that he liked to hang out with on occasion. The girl however was immensely sociable and had multiple groups of friends from different periods of her life – secondary school friends, junior college friends, university friends, cell group friends, university Christian Fellowship friends, CCA[8] friends, etc. And even when they got engaged she wanted to keep up all her social links!

This was tolerable in the beginning of their relationship, but after a while, the guy got seriously annoyed with how her calendar seemed constantly full of other appointments. In fact, he had to book her a week in advance, just to get a timeslot for a date! She began to realise that if this relationship was going to move forward, something would have to give. She would have to reduce the frequency or the number of her social commitments.

When I met them, I suggested that they try to begin to merge their social lives first, and see what happens. That is to say, Jane (the girl) should try to bring Sung (the guy) when she goes out with her friends. There shouldn't be just 'his friends' and 'her friends' any more. They would have to start thinking 'our friends'. Then see how to fit them all in their calendar.

When my wife and I were figuring this out, we decided that generally we would visit all our friends together, as a couple. No more of this 'my friends', 'your friends' business. And just to help our 'trust bank' we made the (some would call it "drastic") decision that generally I would not go out solo with any of my female friends anymore, and neither would she go out with any of her male friends solo anymore. We even got to the state where her male friends would become my friends, and my female friends would now be 'transferred' to her.

Did that work? Yes and no... It depended on the people. And of course, we ended up drifting apart from some friends. But that was the sacrifice we made for each other and we felt it was worth it.

Hobbies

▼ Cut down as many as possible hobbies or church ministries that you are doing on your own. Start doing more things together. Play sports, fix date nights, go on holidays. Take up new church ministries that require both of you to do something together.

▼ Once, you may have played computer games four out of the five hours you were at home. Cut that down to two hours a day at most, and spend the other three hours eating and talking with your wife.

▼ You don't have to give up all your hobbies. But the rule is that anything that annoys the spouse should be considered for the rubbish bin. Anything that emphasises 'me' time above 'us' time really needs to go to the chopping block – or at least be radically trimmed down.

▼ You could agree to join each other in your various hobbies, but it is probably better if you start new hobbies or activities together, otherwise one person will feel like a sacrificial calf!

Ministry

All Christians are encouraged to serve God, whether at church, parachurch ministries, office, home, or all of the above. I believe that if God calls you to get married, God will call you and your spouse to a compatible ministry. I don't believe that the same God who called you to serve in a particular area would make that area of service a source of competition with your spouse.

If you married a non-Christian or not-very-Christian spouse, then yes, by definition, every area of service will be in competition with them, because that is not the direction they want to go.

However, if you both have a goal of growing in Christ then your ministry must match your spouse. This is not to say that you and your spouse should have the same ministry, although that would be nice. For example, volunteering at a soup kitchen together or leading worship together (one singing, one playing the piano). Of course, some ministries have clearly different skill sets that your spouse may not have. But you and your spouse should have compatible ministries[9] and serve in a way that doesn't take too much time away from one another, especially in the early years of marriage.

The worst thing to end up with is to think that serving God and loving your spouse are mutually exclusive. It would be equally terrible if a church advocates service in ministries above serving one's spouse. All that could easily happen if one does not equate loving spouse as a ministry in itself – a ministry which supersedes other ministries!

Physical
Have *sex*!

No, seriously. Have sex. It's amazing how little sex couples have, especially when they are busy with work commitments. Sex is one of the most fundamental ways to affirm your new unity with your bodies. Scripture tells us not to refuse sex if one partner wants it, and to have it often unless it's a special time of prayer.[10]

> *The joy of physical oneness is but an echo of the joy of spiritual oneness with Christ. "The ecstasy and joy of sex is supposed to be a foretaste of the complete ecstasy and joy of total union with Christ,"* is what theologian Tim Keller writes....

> *Physical union is a God-made ceremony to express the exclusivity and intimacy and totality of oneness – and if you use physical intimacy to express anything less than that, you've destroyed its very meaning.*[11]

It is so easy to assume sex will just happen, but in reality you may need to decide with one another to make sure you have sex a certain number of times a week,[12] otherwise it is something that can slip your mind (I know you may think that unbelievable if you are not yet married, but it really can!).

These are some suggestions to get you going. It all sounds pretty brutal – but what do you expect of 'death to self'?

DEATH BEFORE NEW LIFE

As previously mentioned, when two people begin a new life together and they think they can still do everything the same way as before, with the only difference being that they now sleep in the same bed, that's the start of all the trouble. If the guy still wants to have soccer nights and the girl still wants to do her shopping; if the guy still wants to play his computer games and the girl still wants to spend all her time with friends – that's not marriage, that's two different lives.

If they want to get married, they need to start living a whole life together. They need to scrap all that stuff and start again from scratch. They have to rebuild hobbies, plans, goals, restaurant preferences, careers – it's all new because they are now part of something new. They must say a sad farewell to their old way of living and kill it. The more they cling on to their old lives, the more difficult the relationship will be. As long as you are living your old life, you cannot hope to have a great marriage.

In a nutshell, do as many 'together' things as you can in your first year, and as few 'solo' things as you are able. Firm up your relationship. Build and grow it as much as you can! You will need to sacrifice parts of your life that you once did on your own. Blow out your own candle. Yes, it is very painful, very difficult.

But death is absolutely necessary to achieve union. The two ones must first die, before the two can become one. Death before new life, there's no other option.

The more work you put in at the beginning, the more wonderful this marriage will turn out to be in the long run. The longer you drag it out to kill your old life, the more painful this marriage will be, with many problems popping up even 20 or 30 years down the road!

Here's the question – do you believe it's really worth it? Do you know how wonderful a *one* relationship can be when you have chosen and worked with another person until you are beautifully in-sync?

Remember, oneness is a life of fulfilment, of completeness. The closer you get to becoming *one*, the more "one-derful" your life will be (pardon the pun). Why did you get married? Because the life you lived on your own was 'not complete', right? If you want the 'complete' life you must invest in the marriage. The more you 'bank' into this marriage, especially the early credit stage (the first two years), the more you will reap in rewards later on!

Two people coming together can do more than any two people on their own. Is it because they are more productive? No, of course not. Two independent runners on the track would both outpace a three-legged pair. It's like the African proverb that says: "If you want to run fast, run alone. If you want to run far, run together."[13]

Yet it is not simply running together. It is taking the time to work things out to become one, and then watch as the two of you do incredible things together. To sacrifice your life for your marriage is not detrimental – it's highly beneficial to yourself! As Paul pointed out: "He who loves his wife loves himself." (Ephesians 5:28).

Here's what one friend wrote:

> *One must sacrifice himself extravagantly for his bride. In this way – and only in this way – will one love "himself". He'll love "himself" because now, in covenant union, he is one with his bride. There's no solo man anymore. The only way to find himself is to lose himself for her... only because you lose yourself in service of the other and find yourself blessed by that love.*[14]

Because you have said a vow, you are now one new entity. Thus everything you pour into this entity – all the time, money, and energy you spend – will only return back to you. This is your life. Your life includes your spouse.

The converse is also true. Because you are one new entity, all the time, money, and energy you *don't* spend will feedback negatively into your life. Each time you opt for your own choices ahead of your 'together' choices, it adds a little resentment into your spouse and a little distance into your relationship. It will come back to bite you – hard – in the end!

One last thing you may want to do is to introduce new family practices and traditions that are peculiar to the two of you. When you are going to set up a household, you need to think of what will define your household. If you don't think this through, you will simply carry on what your old family did, and this means all the mistakes and failures will be passed on from generation to generation.

Please spend a significant amount of time thinking how you would like to run your new household with your spouse. Make a list of all the practices in your old families that you want to terminate, and the practices that you want to keep on doing.

BEARING FRUIT

So if you've been working on becoming one, how can you know you are truly one? Are there any indicators to tell you that your marriage is going in the right direction?

Indicator 1

One way to tell is when you are 'in' one another. What does that mean? It means that what you do resonates with the other person.

Let's say your spouse gets a promotion, but you don't. Are you happy? Well, his/her promotion means more income and status for both of you, doesn't it? If your first response is joy then you know you are growing in oneness. If your first response is jealousy, that's a good sign that there's work to be done still!

To be one is to be 'in' one another, which means that when something happens to your spouse, it also happens to you, and you feel it in the same way, because you live one life now. If you feel radically different from your spouse, that is a good indication that the closeness has yet to be achieved, and you need to seriously start looking at ways to bring the two of you together. As always, the earlier you do this in marriage, the easier and the more beneficial it is!

The same principle works for your relationship with Jesus, too. He wants you to be 'in Him' and He in you. The faster you take on board His ways and His goals and His church, the easier your Christian walk will be. The more resistant you are to doing His commands, the more drawn out the struggles will be.

Get 'in' there, and get in there fast! It takes a lot of self-death work.

Indicator 2

There's another way to know if you are growing together well: It's about fruit.

When God defined good relationships, He said one way to tell is if they 'bear fruit'. Hence if we 'abide in Jesus' we will bear fruit (John 15). So if we start to be 'in' one another, the outcome is a fruitful relationship.

What is a fruitful relationship? Here's where we go back to the 113 pattern of the Father and the Son.

> ... the Father so enjoyed his fellowship with his Son that he wanted to have the goodness of it spread out and communicated or shared with others. The creation was a free choice borne out of nothing but love.[15]

The Father-Son relationship was so delightful that it resulted in creation. That's what we mean by a fruitful relationship with the love of God. There are all kinds of love, but only one type of love results in a *oneness* that is fruitful. Some relationships can seem to be united but in truth they are horrible!

There was once a story of a one-tonne man on television. This man had eaten so much that he literally weighed one tonne, and they had to use machinery to get him out of the house to have some drastic weight-reduction surgery. They interviewed him and asked how he got like that. His answer was simple enough, "I like to eat." They then asked his wife how she let him get like this. Her answer: "He likes to eat, I like to cook." Now this may look like a beautiful marriage – but they were killing one another. This is not a healthy oneness![16]

The kind of *oneness* that we are talking about is when two people come together so deeply that it becomes like a fountain.

Their love begins to grow and grow as they work out all sorts of different issues, and as they prove that love to one another by making self-sacrifices. One day that love sort of bubbles over and just spills out. The result is always the making of space for others.

Fruitful love makes space. The Father and the Son loved one another so much that humanity was the result. Physical love between husband and wife results in children as the fruit. The love between two bodies grows and grows until it reaches a climax that results in the eventual birth of another person – a child.

Christian marriage is not about two people using one another in a destructive way, but feeding one another, growing one another, and building one another up in such a delightful way that suddenly you find you are so 'built up' that you can handle other people! You become fundamentally stronger as a person with the space to deal with others. That is true fruit.

One result of a fruitful marriage is real, physical children. However, having kids doesn't mean your marriage is going well – it just means you are having sex! But being in a position of fruitful love such that you desire to have kids to lavish that love on and to share that love with does indicate maturity.

Don't have kids because of family pressure, to save face, because it's the 'right thing to do', or because of the law of procreation (whatever that is!). Have children because you have seen the delight one person can bring in marriage and you want to increase that joy exponentially! (Only don't forget that just as it has taken so much work for your marriage to get to the right place, it will also take as much work to bring this new person into your oneness.)

But we're not merely talking about children. Not every couple can have children, for various reasons. We are talking about being so built up in love that you have space for at least spiritual children.

It could be that you adopt, but it could also be that you make space to serve other people who are needier than you. Because your marriage has done so well in building you up, you now have the capacity to help others who are devoid of love and affection.[17]

Fruitful marriages always end up serving others in love together, whether it is through physical or spiritual children.

If you have been married a few years and you find yourselves being more and more selfish, more and more reclusive or cutting yourselves away more and more from family, church and community, then you don't have a healthy oneness. The love between the two of you is not the love of God. It is possibly quite a sickly love. Be very wary of this type of unity! It has the potential to turn a good marriage into something rotten.

WORK FOR THE *ONE*
The most wonderful families I have seen are those that have been through crisis early on in their marital life. They knew they were different people and because of that they made loads of effort to get their marriage right. Some changed jobs, many went for marital enrichment courses, some sought marriage mentors (an older couple to walk alongside them) and others had professional counselling sessions. They knew it wasn't going to be easy, and most importantly they didn't hide their problems, they dealt with them!

After that, what came out was a beautiful marriage. Yet they still insisted on going for marriage classes, date nights, meet-ups with other couples, etc. In fact, when we organise marriage enrichment courses in church, I sometimes get quite annoyed that the only couples who turn up are couples who have successful marriages. But I've learned that the reason they are doing so well is because they keep turning up! They know that it isn't enough to be going for just one counselling session. Rather, they need as much help as they can get for the rest of their lives.

They learned to put aside their individual preferences and listen to one another. They ended up travelling the same path, not just parallel lines – and you can see the fruit of it in their children and in their ministry to others.

What do you want from your marriage?

The goal of marriage is to be *one*.

MARITAL EXERCISE 3
THE CANDLE

Sometime before or just after your marriage, carry out that candle ceremony between the two of you.

Light a candle each, representing your individual lives. Then say to each other, "My life is not my own – it belongs to you."

Use your two candles to light a third candle, and blow out your own candles.

Remember, marriage means death to self. Two becoming one.

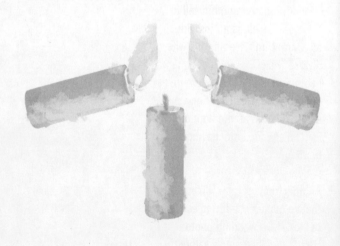

MARITAL EXERCISE 4
WHAT IS BEST FOR THE OTHER?

Becoming one is not something that happens overnight. It takes time to work out issues and ways of thinking over weeks, months and years. But there are things that you can do to proactively think about it.

The best tip I received was from a wise friend who decided that every month or term he was going to take a half-day of leave to go do some 'family thinking'. He would go for a long walk and ask himself, "What is best for my family now?" – first for him and his wife, and then for him, his wife, and their kids.

He was programming himself to no longer think of himself as an individual, but part of a larger unit. He and his wife had very diverse views and temperaments at the beginning of their marriage, but because he made time to constantly put her and their children at the top of his priority list, they ended up having a wonderful marriage!

Another friend of mine did the same, except that he made time during each day at work to look at his wedding photo – to re-centre his mind on his spouse, rather than his job. It gave his job more meaning, too.

Carve out a time slot at least once a month to 'think about the other'. You need to actually book some leave – the costlier the time, the better! Take a walk, talk to a mentor, go some place where you can think and pray.

Ask yourself, "What does my family need? What does my spouse need at this moment in time?" Make decisions there and then to change small things or even big directions according to what is best for your new family unit.

This is something I guarantee you will never regret!

MARITAL EXERCISE 5
DESIGNING A HOUSEHOLD

Spend some time thinking through what kind of household you would want to create.

As mentioned, you can list out things you liked about your old household, e.g. we had family dinners once a week, we made an effort to talk to the neighbours, we would pray together each night before we slept, mum decided that she would be a stay-home mum, we made birthdays important, etc.

Also list out things you didn't like about your old household, e.g. we watched television while we ate, dad never talked to us personally, we always went straight to our rooms when we came home, we never served in church together, we were never generous with money, etc.

After that, make a list of new things you would like to have in your household, e.g. a new Christmas Eve tradition, a date night, a new sport, family board games night, yearly holidays to a fixed destination, serving regularly at a welfare organisation, certain values or life principles, etc. It doesn't matter what it is, as long as it is something meaningful for the both of you as you begin living together – and later, for your children, too.

After that, come up with some sort of written family statement: "This is what we want our household to be like – we want to be Jesus centred, neighbourly, and family focused, which means…" (you fill in the blanks).

Get your new household going with a purpose and come back every year to review the written statement to assess how you are going, or even to change some priorities as you both grow and mature.

Don't just amble along with family life – make it purposeful!

CHAPTER 6
A DANCE FOR TWO

So far we've understood that marriage involves two people locked in covenant relationship for life. Marriage happens when a vow is said.

Secondly, we've established that the goal of marriage is that two different persons need to work to become one.

Now thirdly, we want to get into the fact that becoming one doesn't mean becoming the same. Although the goal is to become one in heart, mind, will, direction, ambition, etc., two people are always going to be two distinct people, with *different roles* to play.

Going back to the 113 pattern: In the Father-Son relationship, there are two Persons who are one. Yet the two Persons are always distinct. The Father never becomes the Son, and the Son never becomes the Father. Union does not abolish their Personhood. Unity does not get rid of their distinction as unique Persons. Also, the two Persons are equal (as is the Spirit). The Father is God, the Son is God. The Father is not 'more God' than the Son, or vice versa.

So we can see that our pattern for relationship is two distinct persons, who are always equal, coming together to become one. Likewise in marriage, the husband and wife are equal persons – neither is more *significant* than the other. But there is a difference in the two persons:

> But I want you to understand that the head of every man is Christ, the head of a wife is her husband, and the head of Christ is God.
> (1 Corinthians 11:3)

There are roles. In the Trinity, the Father is the Head and Christ is the Body. In the gospel, Christ is the Head and the church is the Body. In marriage, the husband is the Head and the wife is the Body.

There are different roles for the husband and wife to play. They are both equal, but they have different roles to play to allow this relationship to become one. The roles help us to achieve oneness.

NOT INTERCHANGEABLE

All organisations, in order to run smoothly, need to assign different roles to people.

Imagine a large company where everyone was CEO – that would be a disaster. Who would do the administration? Who would do the accounting? Who would run the programmes? Who would clean the floor? Nothing would work at all!

In every association of two or more people, if things are going to work, each must have a role to play. So it is with the church. It is described as one body, with many members.[1] And each member needs to play his/her role well in order for the whole body to function – to do its purpose of proclaiming Jesus Christ as Lord to the church. If one part neglects or denies his/

her role, the whole body suffers!

Yet even in an organisation, we don't just assign roles to people any-old-how. It's not that you get hired and then pick a lottery ball that tells you your assigned role. No, it's clear that different people are differently talented for different tasks.

In the Trinity, the Father, Son, and Spirit never swap roles. The Father is eternally the Father and loves to be the Father. The Son is eternally the Son and loves to be His Father's Son.[2] The Spirit seems to never desire to be either Father or Son, and is very happy working in the background.

Likewise, when we were made, all of us were made with non-interchangeable roles. Even in the church, it's not that we randomly pick our area of service. We may do so in the beginning. But later on we will find that we are suited for different roles in comparison with the other members of the church. And we base that suitability on our 'design'. We are different by design.

Our roles are built in to us by our Creator, by the Spirit of God.[3] *Our job is not to pick our role, but to figure out what we already have in-built within us.*

The faster we figure it out, the better we can get into our niche in the church and in the world. We will find that we are more effective because we know what we have been designed to do. As one author aptly put it, "You can't be anything you want to be".[4]

In the church, we need to accept that we have been created in a certain way, figure out how we've been designed, and then utilise our gifts and talents, putting them into practice. When all that happens, first of all we will feel fulfilled as persons (we will know who we are meant to be), and secondly, the body will work marvellously!

Roles are deeply tied to our own sense of self-worth and fulfilment, and are required for any two or more persons to be able to work together. So it is within a marriage. Each gender is designed differently:

> *Our genders are not created by ourselves but by God. Gender has a deep aspect of identity, not a disposable outfit we tailor to taste.*[5]

Within covenent marriage, each gender has a different role to play:

> *There is a certain male-ness to men and female-ness to women, and when they enter into a certain kind of one-ness (that is marriage), they are meant to flow in a certain way.*[6]

Roles don't make one person less equal to another. Roles distinguish equal persons from one another. Roles help both persons function together better.

Do you believe that you were designed to play a certain role in the church? Do you believe that you were designed in gender to play a certain role in marriage?

It requires a mindset change!

DIFFERENT BY DESIGN
Even without being married. It is clear that boys and girls are created differently. But what would you say are the differences between men and women outside of marriage?

In Scripture there is a hint: "… the woman as the weaker vessel… (1 Peter 3:7)".

Biologically, this is fairly obvious. There are clearly differences in the physiology of men and women, the most obvious one being that women are designed to have children (generally speaking) and men are not. It is also generally true that women are physically weaker, having less muscle mass and a higher fat percentage.[7]

But it also seems there are other differences:

> ... the men should pray, lifting holy hands without anger or quarrelling... women should adorn themselves in respectable apparel, with modesty and self-control, not with braided hair and gold or pearls or costly attire... (1 Timothy 2:8-9)

Some Christian counsellors have suggested that according to verses like the above, men are designed to be more 'expressive' and women to be more 'receptive' (biologically this is also true).[8]

Hence in 1 Timothy, the author knows that men are much more prone to things like quarrelling – where men's expressiveness has gone wrong. And women would be much more prone to wanting to be noticed in the wrong way – their receptivity gone wrong. In Genesis 3, the curse when applied to men implies that men will abuse a relationship by becoming tyrants, whereas women would abuse a relationship by being seductresses.[9]

Not wanting to get into too much detail here, but clearly Scripture acknowledges key differences in design when it comes to men and women. Only in general terms, of course, for all men and women can become children of God, and accomplish great things and have a purpose. In fact, all are the same when it comes to their relationship in Christ:

> *There is neither Jew nor Greek, there is neither slave nor free, there is neither male nor female, for you are all one in Christ Jesus. (Galatians 3:28)*

Statements like this do not deny that different races, social status, and genders exist, but rather, despite the differences, all are seen as equal in reference to their status in Jesus. In fact in Galatians, it is implied that we are to treat each other equally simply as Christians – not to view anyone 'according to the flesh'.[10]

However, what we want to emphasise is that different roles come into play once people are within an 'organisation'. As an individual your gifts are unimportant in terms of your worth or your standing, but in the church, your gifts are important with respect to your role and function. Similarly, in marriage, you are equal persons, with equal standing before God, but now that you are in a covenantal arrangement, your roles do matter. In fact, they matter incredibly!

TIME FOR A LITTLE ROLE PLAY

> *Husband-wife roles and their impact on power or influence in marriage frequently become an issue during premarital counselling. I find that most couples do not go into sufficient detail in the area of roles.*[11]

If for the rest of your life you are being defined by your oneness with one another, then your role becomes tied to your identity for the rest of your life – until one of you dies. Then the role stops. The Father and the Son of course have eternally bound roles that define them.

If one does not learn and come to terms with the roles to play, then this life-long partnership is going to resemble a body that is functioning terribly, or an organisation gone wrong from the very beginning.

What then is the role of a husband and wife?

Let's do a little exercise. Let's take several New Testament passages that tell us about husbands and try to build up a description of his role in relation to his wife:

- ▼ Ephesians 5: Head, love, sacrifice, sanctify, cleanse, present, don't hate, nourish, cherish, hold fast
- ▼ Colossians 3: Love, don't be harsh
- ▼ 1 Peter 3: Understand, honour

Now let's do the same with the wife in relation to the husband:

- ▼ Ephesians 5: Submit, body, respect
- ▼ Colossians 3: Submit
- ▼ 1 Peter 3: Be subject, respectful, pure, gentle and quiet spirit, obey

You will realise that the husband is to be like the Father to the Son, is to be like Christ to the church, which means:

The husband is to lead and love his wife, sacrificing himself for her to make her into the most beautiful woman (especially on the inside) possible. He is to cherish her and help her grow, not be harsh to her. He is to do his best to try to understand her and always honour her. As the head of the family, he is ultimately responsible for everything in the family, whether spiritual, emotional, financial, or physical issues.

The wife is to be like the Son to the Father, like the church to Christ, the body to the head: The wife is to submit to the husband in his leadership. She is to trust that all he is doing is a sacrifice for her benefit and beauty. As one theologian said, she is to "affirm, receive and nurture"[12] her husband's leadership and strength, respecting him as the head of the household.

Now how exactly you and your spouse try to work out the specific dynamics of these roles is a whole different story. What these roles *do not* mandate is the traditional pattern of the husband working and the wife staying at home to take care of the children. Now that may be a preference that you wish to carry out – most certainly that is what my wife and I have done – but that is *not* implied within those role statements.

This is what my good friend once wrote:

> *In many circumstances, the roles in Head/Body relationships can be inter-changeable. But there's a deep 'direction of travel'... If we deny the direction of travel, then the relationship doesn't go where it's supposed to.*
>
> *Freeze-frame a marriage at any one point and either spouse might look like the active partner, either spouse might look like they are 'taking a lead'... We just can't insist on one kind of action for one member of the relationship. In fact, to worry about specifics is a big mistake. Having roles is about having an overall shape to the relationship in which the Head serves in love and the Body encourages and receives that serving love. And when this shape is even approximated in human marriages, something wonderful happens... It's a beautiful thing when true roles are played out.*[13]

The role statements only imply a way of relating to one another, summed up in the husband leading the wife in self-sacrificial loving decisions, and the wife trusting the husband and affirming him.

Now this doesn't come naturally! As we need to learn how to use our gifts, so it is with our roles.

First we need to acknowledge what they are. Secondly, we need to learn how to think that way. And thirdly, we need to figure out how exactly they will be expressed in every situation of married life from now on – which will be a continual process. But the direction of Head and Body never change.

LEARNING TO DANCE

Let's think of a ballroom dance, where two persons come together to create something beautiful. Now the first time you two come together, it's not likely that you're going to be able to follow the music naturally. It will probably be the most painful experience you've ever had! You may come away with bruised shins and bleeding toes. But if you do want to dance, you need to learn your role – your part!

In ballroom dancing, there is always the leading partner. Two people cannot lead! Someone has to begin the rotation or the next step, but the other partner is not passive – she has to follow and to receive the movement. If the leading partner does not push, then nothing happens. If the receiving partner does not accept the push, then everyone falls down!

The better the dance you want to create, the more you need to learn your role, and the more you need to be responsive to each other.

THE LEADING PARTNER

> *I, soon-to-be-husband, take you, lady, as my wedded wife, to have and to hold, from this day forward, for better for worse, for richer for poorer, in sickness and in health, to love, **to lead** and to cherish…*

This is what I once said to a bridegroom on his wedding day:

> *Sam, you need to lead. Now this doesn't mean that the husband says "jump" and the wife says "yes dear, how high". To be the head of a Christian marriage – means to be the one responsible for love. To be the husband in a marriage means to be the one responsible to make sure that there is love in the family.*
>
> *That means, when things aren't going well, when your wife feels down, when the work situation is miserable, when the finances are running dry, and you all feel horrible. Sam, you must be the one to introduce love back into the family. Sam, you must be the source*

of love flowing into the family. You must be the one to pick up your wife, to work through the finances, to find another job, to look for a house, you must be the one to show to your wife and any potential children that you love them – no matter what is happening. You must be the one to find a way to make your family smile in times of darkness – that is your role. That is what it means to lead.

Jesus does not just love us with any kind of love. He loves us with a love that transforms us. He says that He loves us with a love that makes us holy. Holy is a word that in my opinion just means beautiful. He loves us to make us beautiful – He loves us to make us into the best people that we ever could be, people who are gentle, kind, patient, caring, and full of love for others – just like Jesus. Beautiful people.

As Christ loves you Sam, and is making you beautiful, it is now your job to love your wife and make her beautiful. You need to love her in such a way that she feels beautiful from the inside out. How does that work?

Well, whenever she feels like she hasn't done well in her job, you love her – you tell her that she's the best. Whenever others tell her they don't value her, you love her – you show her in very practical ways how much you value her. Whenever she feels like she hasn't been a good wife or spouse or mother, you love her – you tell her, even if it's for the 100th time, that you would never

> want to be with anyone else. She's the best woman you have ever known.
>
> You make her so secure in your love that she feels like the queen of England. And as she knows she is loved so much by you, she will feel beautiful, and she will do the most wonderful things in your marriage, and in her life. She will be like a beautiful lily, opening up for all the world to see. As a good friend of mine was told just before his wedding day, "Don't love her because she is beautiful, love her to make her beautiful."
>
> Because it is when you are doing that, that you are loving her like Jesus loves you. Jesus loves His church with a love so powerful – being in His love feels like you are being bathed in sunshine – it transforms us, opening us up into beautiful blossoming lilies. Jesus keeps telling His church that she is beautiful, and because of that, she really does become beautiful. Love your wife to make her beautiful. That's your role.

That was my summary of the role of the husband.

It is not going to be natural for a husband to lead out of self-sacrificial love. It will be much more natural for a husband either to lead tyrannically and become an abusive boss, or to completely give up his role and opt to become a passive couch potato. But husbands, just remember this one verse:

> In the same way husbands should love their wives as their own bodies. He who loves his wife loves himself. (Ephesians 5:28)

Because of the fact that you are one, to love your wife is to love yourself!

Remember, the more you invest in your wife, the more comes back to you. The more you show her that you are doing everything for her, interested in her, desirous of her physically, emotionally, mentally, and spiritually – even jealous for her[14] – the more she will trust you and shower love back to you.

In the 113 pattern, the Father loves to glorify the Son, to put Him on a pedestal, give Him the best and most challenging jobs, make Him perfect. But even as the Father does so, the Son in turn glorifies the Father and everyone ends up knowing how awesome a Dad He is!

So it is with husband and wife: "… but woman is the glory of man" (1 Corinthians 11:7b). As you glorify your wife (that is to say, let the world know how wonderful she is), she will glorify you (people will know how awesome you are). Ultimately, to love your wife sacrificially is indeed to have that love returned to yourself. He who loves his wife loves himself, remember that!

It works negatively as well. He who doesn't love his wife hates his own body. Therefore, he hates himself, does harm to himself, and destroys himself. Remember that, too!

Do you know that the most common complaint from older women is the passivity of their husband? It is one of the greatest problems. But it is the fault of both dance partners. If you want your husband to lead, he must first have the mindset of leadership and you too must have the mindset of encouraging him to lead. It works both ways.

If you try to neutralise the roles, then most certainly he won't lead – and he'll be very happy to melt into the couch once again. But if the man accepts his leadership role and the woman affirms him, something beautiful begins to happen. Sure, there will be a lot of bruised toes in the beginning, but eventually, the dance will begin to take shape.

Let's think again about the dance. Imagine you have a very passive dance leader. He does not want to take the initiative in your moves. Now the wrong thing to do is to take the leadership role out of his hands. He will just become a useless dance partner. In fact, he will become dead weight – a henpecked husband. And you won't look very attractive either.

So what can you do?

You can *pull instead of push*. Give him little nudges and create the space for him to lead. Leave things undone and undecided and wait for him. This kind of submissive 'action' can do amazing things! Peter says it can even have the potential to convert non-Christians:

> *Likewise, wives, be subject to your own husbands, so that even if some do not obey the word, they may be won without a word by the conduct of their wives, when they see your respectful and pure conduct. (1 Peter 3:1-2)*

Jesus used this kind of gentle submissiveness to win over the world. Quiet strength shown in purposeful submission is the most powerful force out there. In the Sermon on the Mount, Jesus implies that it can convert even the hardest of hearts.[15] Never underestimate the power of 'active submission'.

I always suggest to newlywed women that the best thing they can do for their marriage is to compel their husbands to lead – not by nagging – but by being cunning. Always allow him to think he came up with ideas or plans or activities even when it was really your idea. It will give him confidence and he will be able to lead and love in a way that you never dreamed of. Now what if the husband loves, but the wife doesn't want to follow? Well, I think Jesus knows that all too well with us. Just keep loving until she sees there's something worth following.

THE FOLLOWING PARTNER

> *I, soon-to-be-wife, take you, gentleman, as my wedded husband, to have and to hold, from this day forward, for better for worse, for richer for poorer, in sickness and in health, to love, to cherish **and to submit in the Lord**…*

It isn't going to be natural for a woman to accept her submissive role as well. After all, all of us have submission issues. It's not so easy for us to submit to our bosses – hence everyone wants to be an independent businessman. It's not so easy to submit to even Jesus Christ – what more a fallible man as a husband.

At that same wedding, this is what I said to the bride:

> *And Gwen, what is your role? Your role in this marriage is to submit. That means you are to receive Sam's love. Isn't that a great role? To receive this love?*
>
> *But it's harder than it sounds. To receive Sam's love, means you must learn to trust him. You must trust that every decision Sam makes is done because he loves you and is doing it for your benefit. And that is a hard thing to do. It is not so easy to trust your life into someone's hands.*

In some sense, Gwen, you are leaving everything you have to follow Sam. It will involve changing your whole life. Now some might say, "Aw… So romantic… She's getting whisked away by a dashing young man who swept her off her feet." But we're Singaporean, we aren't so romantic. We'll probably be thinking, "Eh, why like that, then your career how, your family how?"

See, Gwen has got to trust that all those decisions Sam is making are not just to advance his career, his life, but they are the best decisions for her too.

Do you know when Sam proposed, they were taking a stroll when he asked her this question: "Will you let me take care of you for the rest of your life?" And Gwen said, "Yes."

That is the question for you every day of your marriage, Gwen. Will you trust Sam, let him lead you, and take care of you for the rest of your life? You said yes that day, but there will be days you will think, "Did I make the right decision or not? What am I doing in this place, I don't know anyone, what am I doing here?" There will be many times you will be tempted to not trust him, to not go along with his decisions, to not receive his love.

But let me tell you a secret, just between you and me, okay? As a husband, I'm secretly hoping my wife will not trust me. You know why? Because if my wife doesn't trust me,

> *and decides to make all her own decisions… Good – then I don't have to bother taking care of her, thinking about her, worrying about her and how's she's feeling. I don't have to bother loving her.*
>
> *Do you get it? The more you don't let him lead you, the less he will have to love you. If you want him to love you more, let him lead, give him the responsibility, make him take the d ecisions. I tell you, by doing that you will stress him out so much, that he will run to Jesus to get as much love as possible to make sure he fulfils his promise – to take care of you for the rest of his life.*
>
> *Gwen, let him lead. It will be the best decision you ever make.*

Yes, it is true that submission itself is hard, let alone submission to someone who can fail. But that does not mean the solution is not to submit. The solution is to learn to submit despite the failing! The hope is that the more you show your willingness to trust and follow, the more the leading partner will be motivated and spurred to take up a sacrificial role for your benefit.

In some sense it is the same instinct that works in both mothers and fathers to be good parents. When we see a child willing to hang on to our every word, even the worst of humans can be motivated to want to do the best for them – even to change for them.

I'm most certainly not saying that wives = children. Truth be told, you are likely to be much smarter than your husband! But I am saying that if you want this relationship to work, if you want the whole thing to run smoothly, if you want to bring out the best in him for your sake (and the children's sakes), then let him lead.

The great temptation from the woman's side is that she does not follow. You know what happens to a dance when one partner does not follow? Everyone falls down. Or worse, you end up not dancing together at all.

Another temptation is to follow without thought, to simply do whatever the husband says without thinking or wanting to know why he's doing it. This sort of passive following is just as bad as the passive husband. It indicates that neither party is actually interested in one another.

Very often in marriages, the wife can sometimes be resigned to her role of submission, and the whole relationship ends up becoming "You say what… I do what". That's Singaporean for "I will just do whatever you say without thought or feeling". If this progresses, it inevitably leads to a very resentful spirit within the wife, who ends up grumbling on the inside and gossiping on the outside.

Wives, you need to be very wary of this spirit. It will kill your marriage and has the potential to turn your husband into a tyrant when you are younger, and turn you into a vicious gossip when you are older.

Actually, all of us need be very wary about this spirit. Once a relationship gets to the stage where we are just doing our 'jobs' – our assigned roles – without any thought, communication, or willingness to work with and for the other, that is a true indication that the relationship is dying. "You do this, I do that… And we don't disturb one another" means the relationship is over!

We need to work out our roles with one another and learn to enjoy them. To submit does not mean to say how high when he says jump. It means to trust that he has your best interests at heart. To do that would require a lot of effort on your part to listen, understand, clarify, debate for the sake of clarity, offer counter-opinions, nurture, affirm, compromise, etc. It does not come automatically.

DANCE PRACTICE
These things need to be thought through and learned. In fact, the church is specifically instructed to *teach* these roles to one another:

> *Older women likewise are to… train the young women to love their husbands and children. (Titus 2:3-4)*

No one ever thought it would come naturally! Older husbands need to teach younger husbands and older wives need to teach younger wives how to play their new roles. We need to learn willingly from other people.

Here's a question, though: What happens in a marriage where the husband is not so smart, not earning much, an introvert, etc., and the wife is smarter, older, paid more, clearly more capable, outspoken, etc.?

Let me tell you the story of a couple I know:

> Harry was a senior student in university where he met the girl of his dreams, Sally. His friends were delighted when he told them the news. However, their delight turned to looks of abject horror when they found out that that 'girl' was actually his direct boss in the company that he was interning at!

Harry, however, was not fazed. He was determined to follow his heart. After all she was a committed Christian, too, and he firmly believed that loving Jesus was the only criteria that he needed to find in a life-partner (assuming she was single, of course).

Time passed, Harry graduated, and they got together! She was still his boss, and he was the company's newest employee.

Eventually they got married. Things were great at the wedding… but then went immediately downhill once life together began. She was clearly smarter, more highly paid (much more!) and more senior than he was in every respect.

She was the one who paid for their house. She was the one who could afford all the furniture. She was the one who knew how to live a more disciplined life while he was a bit all over the place. A bit juvenile, she thought.

Strain began to show in their marriage, but they were both determined to work it out. They could have decided to just aspire to be 'equal partners', but they both knew it wouldn't work out. After all, she was way more mature than he was.

They could have decided that she would lead the marriage and he would follow – that could have been a potential solution, but there was a problem. That isn't the way God desires marriage to be. He wants the husband to lead and the wife to follow, in order to reflect the gospel of Christ and the church. They knew it, believed it, and wanted whole-heartedly to follow it.

So they began the arduous process of Harry 'manning up' and Sally 'womaning up'. They went for counselling, and he took up the lead in decisions – including financial decisions. She made much more money, but he would decide how to use it.

This was tough. He often bought what she called 'toys' with the money. He had to show her that he was going to use 'her' money for their benefit! He learned the hard way; she learned to trust. This then spilled over into other areas, especially spiritual leadership, where he talked to other more mature men for advice on how to lead the family. He got himself involved in a men's group to improve his own spiritual growth as well.

It took about two years, but at the end of it, their friends could see a difference in their marital dynamics – and it was wonderful! Their marriage was much stronger, like something forged out of the furnace of difficulty. They had a child soon after and their ideas of parenting again proved to be a minor battleground, but it wasn't as critical, because the pattern of the husband being the Head and the wife being the Body was already established. Their new family was doing well.

I want to emphasise again that in the 113 pattern the husband and wife are equal, just like the Father and Son are equal, but they are designed for specific roles.

Remember, the roles are not interchangeable. If we do not fulfil these roles, there are real consequences. It is not just that the marriage suffers – there are also spiritual consequences:

> *Likewise, husbands, live with your wives in an understanding way, showing honour to the woman as the weaker vessel, since they are heirs with you of the grace of life, so that your prayers may not be hindered.*
> *(1 Peter 3:7)*

Peter implies that if husbands do not honour their wives, their prayers will be hindered. In this passage, Peter has been talking about how both husband and wife have opportunities to display the gospel to one another. The wife can display the gospel to her husband by showing that she is willing to submit to him precisely because she submits to Jesus Christ. The husband can display the gospel to his wife by showing that he is willing to honour her – affirming that although she is submitting to him, yet she too is an equal heir of this 'grace of life' that is found in Jesus Christ.

Our prayers are answered insofar as they are aligned to the will of God. Hence, if a husband domineers over his wife, or if a wife does not submit to her husband, then it is likely that we do not understand the purposes of God. Hence our prayers will be "hindered", for it is unlikely that we are praying according to His will. This shows how seriously God takes these roles once you've entered into covenant marriage.

The more both husband and wife accept their roles and try to live out the general shape of these roles, the more you will find the freedom and flexibility in this relationship. Two professional dance partners can create all kinds of magic once they completely trust each other.

Like a well-oiled machine, each person in an organisation needs to know his/her part. The better you know your part, the better everything functions, and the greater the accomplishments.

Remember that you were designed for these roles by your created gender. What's supposed to happen is that when everything works together, you will feel most fulfilled as a person, despite what society has programmed you to think.

RESONANCE

When both husband and wife are working within the mindset of their pre-designed roles, the result is harmony.

It is what happens when persons come together to be one. It's like the music that comes from an orchestra or a choir. When you have one finely tuned instrument or voice, it is beautiful. However, when you have many instruments or voices all finely tuned you can significantly increase the beauty and complexity of the symphony.

Harmony requires differences coming together. Uniformity cannot generate symphony. The different roles are key.

Different notes coming together create a phenomenon called resonance, where the whole is greater than the sum of its parts. Each person amplifies the other, creating something deeper, richer, and more glorious than one could do on his or her own.

It also works in culinary terms: Professional chefs know that different ingredients are not meant to mask each other – we're not supposed to drown our meats in condiments. But the true skill of cooking is when different ingredients amplify one another, bringing out the deep flavours in each other, and complementing one another. Beef tastes beefier, vegetables become crunchier, fish becomes less fishy,[16] etc.

That is resonance. It is the goal of becoming one, to become more than you could ever be when you were alone.

This is from my wedding sermon to another couple:

> *Please discern the will of the Lord for your family. Previously you asked what God wanted you to do with your lives as individuals, now you must ask Him again what He wants you to do as a family. He will have a new calling for your* ***third way of life.***
>
> *As you work in your separate jobs, you are no longer working for your own bank accounts. Work together for a common purpose, a common mission. God will tell you what it is, and it will involve the both of you, as well as any children God may bless you with. Spend much time asking Him. I'm pleading with you, don't just jump back into life as it was before this day. Let this wedding day be remembered. Let it make a more profound impact on your lives than simply living under one roof.*

This is not just the goal of marriages; it is also the goal of the church and it is the very life of God. The reason that Jesus can accomplish so much is because He is one with the Father, and that union allows Him to do everything.

So it is with the church – with Christ we can do everything. And so it should be with husbands and wives. You can do more together than you could ever do by yourself.

The more you play your roles, the more your oneness will be seen and realised. You will increasingly be fulfilled as persons since you are playing the part you were designed to play.

But all of this requires a change in mindset. All of this requires *work, learning, and practice*. All of this requires self-sacrifice.

What would you expect from two new dance partners wanting to win a championship tournament? Expect no less of marriage. The work is hard, but the outcome is stunning, beautiful, and glorious!

NOT ALONE
One final point: Remember that you are not alone in this journey. You should have your church community around you. Peers to journey with you and mentors to help guide you. It is the duty of the whole church to make sure that *every* marriage works: "Let marriage be held in honor among *all*…" (Hebrews 13:4a, emphasis mine).

Go for counselling if you need help. Go for regular enrichment courses to get regular reminders and tips. Talk to your brothers and sisters in Christ to share your joys and your struggles. Remind yourselves of what the Scriptures say when you have forgotten why you got married in the first place.

And in the end, you will indeed learn to dance. And dance you shall, creating something beautiful!

MARITAL EXERCISE 6
ROLE PLAY

Take some time to affirm each other in your roles.

Speak these phrases to each other:

> "I affirm you as my husband. You are the Head of our new household. Your role is to lead this family in self-sacrificial love, to honour, to cherish, to nourish, to cleanse, and to beautify me, your wife, and our children. I choose to submit to you."

> "I affirm you as my wife. You are the Body of our new household. Your role is to submit in quietness and trust in my leadership, despite my failings. I accept my role to lead our family in love for your benefit, not my own. Help me to lead by strengthening and affirming my hands and heart."

CHAPTER 7
THE FINAL WORD

So far, we've tried to alter our marriage mindset by looking at the Trinitarian relationship between the Father and the Son, as well as the parallel relationship between Christ and the church.

We've seen that:

1. The basis of marriage is the **vow**.
2. The goal of marriage is **oneness**.
3. There are **roles** in marriage.

However, there is something different between the husband-wife relationship in comparison with the other two relationships. And it is reflected in the marital questions and vows:

> … *as long as you both shall live?*
> … *till death do us part.*

The difference is death. The husband-wife relationship is only a temporal relationship. The Father-Son relationship and the Christ-church relationship are eternal ones.

So it creates a bit of a problem – how will you deal with *death*?

Some people have suggested that this creates a lose-lose situation: If the marriage does not go well, you lose (obviously). If the marriage *does* go well, you lose, too – because in the end, someone ends up dying. And naturally, the stronger the marriage relationship, the more painful the separation! How does that make you feel?

One day, you will most certainly lose your spouse to the grave. That may be the worst day of your life and it will create a wound in you that may never entirely heal. No wonder Tennyson wrote, "'Tis better to have loved and lost / Than never to have loved at all".

THE FINAL MINDSET

Death – this is where we go back to the place we first began. It's all about the mindset. If you went into marriage thinking that this is the be all and end all of all life, you will end up being sorely disappointed when marriage does not match your expectations. Or you will be in great despair when you lose a spouse who was indeed beginning to fulfil you in ways you never thought possible.

What is the original purpose of marriage? It is to show you the God who created marriage – the Father-Son (in the Spirit) relationship. It is to point you to the gospel – that you are invited to join Christ in marriage.

If you remember that this is the point of marriage and design your marriage to fit that pattern, then you will be in a better position to handle death. The *only eternal lesson* of earthly marriage is to encourage you and others to join the heavenly marriage. Through your success in marriage, you and others around you will see what Jesus Christ offers us in the gospel and what kind of God the Father is. This is the ultimate purpose of every single marriage, especially the Christian ones!

If we look at Scripture, we find that this is nothing new. God's purpose is the same for all the good gifts that He gives to us. He gives us bread so that we may discover the True Bread in Jesus Christ. Even as we enjoy the wonderful gift of bread, we have to see beyond bread to understand that what we truly need is the Living Bread who came down from Heaven. So it is with the gift of marriage. We are to enjoy it rightly now, and one day we will enjoy the True Marriage that is to come.

So when things go well in your marriage, give thanks, and remind yourselves that the True Marriage will be better! When things don't go well in your marriage, pray and ask the Lord for help to resolve the problems – and know that the True Bridegroom will be better!

Remember, as you say your vows, that the goal of this marriage is to point you to God and the gospel. If not, you will be destroyed when you lose your spouse, and you will blame God for the loss.

My friends, as much as marriage means you *must* go *all in* to have a successful marriage, you must also remember that you go into earthly marriage so that you can go into heavenly marriage. That is why the Bible does not recommend that all get married and even implies that if you can, stay single. In other words, if you are already experiencing the benefits of the Christ-church marriage, then just stick with that marriage![1]

Ideally, after a life-long marriage and your spouse dies, although you are indeed free to re-marry and create a new covenant union, my guess is it seems preferable that through the first marriage, you'd understand what eternity would be like with your Heavenly Bridegroom, so now you can devote the rest of your life to serving Him.

Marriage is here to help us heal, to help us learn. But it is here only as a sign, to point us to the heavenly marriage.

Let me make this clear – you *will not* be married to your spouse in heaven.[3] In the new creation, all of us will be brothers and sisters married to our one true Husband – Jesus.

That's it.

Let me end with something else I said to Sam and Gwen:

> *You know, Gwen, I've got some sad news for you. As much as Sam will try to love you, one day, that love will disappear. Death will take Sam from you. You will say this in your vows – your marriage is till death do us part. But there is one type of love that is stronger than death.*
>
> *[to the congregation] Do you know that Sam and Gwen have inscribed Bible verses on their wedding rings? This is the verse on Sam's ring – it's from a book in the Bible called "The Greatest Song Ever" and it goes like this:*
>
>> Set me as a seal upon your heart, as a seal upon your arm, for love is strong as death, jealousy is fierce as the grave. Its flashes are flashes of fire, the very flame of the LORD. Many waters cannot quench love, neither can floods drown it. If a man offered for love all

the wealth of his house, he would be utterly despised. (Song of Solomon 8:6-7)

Sam chose this verse because I think he wants to be reminded that there is a kind of love that is as strong as death, as fierce as the grave; a kind of love that many waters cannot quench, that floods cannot drown; a kind of love that even if a man offered his whole wealth – it would be worthless in comparison. And that is the love that Jesus Christ has for His people, His bride. He loves us with a love stronger than death, and His love, unlike our marriages, will go beyond the grave…. For even when we die, his love will reach down all the way into the grave and call us back to life, so that we can be with Him forever. He's never going to let us go, and nothing will separate us from His love.

Gwen, Jesus will never stop loving you.

There is only *one love* stronger than death, and this is what it looks like:

Please, do all you can to make your marriage work. For it is then that you will understand what kind of life you can expect with the God who created marriage. But please, do not come under the illusion that this marriage will last forever!

CHAPTER 8
A SUMMARY

Marriage is a relationship between a man and a woman, which is based on the relationship between Christ and the church, which itself is based on the relationship between the Father and the Son.

This is the 113 pattern.

It means that the goal in marriage is to testify to the Father-and-Son relationship – and therefore to display the gospel in Christ, through marriage, to the world.

From the 113 pattern we learn that:

1. Marriage is a covenant union between two people making a free choice to love one another. They seal that choice by making a vow, a promise: "I will love you no matter what." Divorce must never be considered as it is something extremely harmful.

2. In marriage, there is the formation of a new 'one'. A unity between two different but equal persons in body – "the two will become one flesh" – hoping to become one in mind, will, and heart. It is a prioritised relationship that supersedes all other relationships (except the one between you and God). It is a oneness that is meant to bear much fruit.

3. In marriage, each person has non-interchangeable roles assigned to him/her by the Father who created them. The husband is called to love, nourish, cherish, and self-sacrifice for his wife. The wife is called to submit and respect her husband; to adorn herself with a quiet and gentle spirit. The two persons are different but come together in a dance-like harmony to create something beautiful.

4. Since earthly marriage is only a reflection of the true marriage between the church and Christ, it is destined to pass away at death – "till death do us part". That's when the true marriage to the Bridegroom comes into its fullness.

APPENDIX A
CONFLICT RESOLUTION

Here's a little afterthought about one of the big issues of marriage – conflict resolution.

As we are working through our journey of marriage and practising our new mindset, there will be many hiccups and all-out fistfights with our spouses along the way. Many people have given different ways and strategies to handle conflicts as they arise, such as:

1. Settle all scores before bedtime.

2. If there's an outstanding issue, fix a time and place where you will have a dedicated conversation about it.

3. Put up a 'red flag' to indicate if now is not the time to deal with something, but a 'white flag' when it is the time to do so!

4. Make sure you settle one issue at a time before another one arises, otherwise it's very easy to make each new argument about every past issue since the relationship began. Some people call this 'becoming historical'.[1]

5. Understand each other's styles of dealing with conflict. Some people like to get some fresh air, others like to ponder over things deeply first, still others like to settle things immediately. If you don't know each other's styles, you will assume the worst of the other person even when they are not trying to be difficult, but rather trying to deal with it in their own way.

These are all excellent ways of dealing with conflict.

However, the problem with most conflicts is not the methodology. It is the motivation. It's not the 'How?' but the 'Why should I?' that is the problem! What we need when arguments arise is a *reason* to solve the problem.

We've already given some reasons – the locked room and the 'he who loves his wife loves himself' logic. Scripture has a few others in dealing with any conflict in general, not just marital conflict:

▼ **Matthew 5:21-26**. When two brothers are angry with one another they should settle it quickly. But more than that, to go to the altar. We need to be reminded of the forgiveness that God has given us at the cross before we are able and motivated to forgive another person who may have sinned against us (or vice versa). When we go to do something for God He will remind us to sort out our issues with one another.

▼ **Philippians 4:2-7**. When two sisters were upset with one another, Paul reminded them that what they needed to do was to remember the joy in the Lord: "Rejoice in the Lord always; again I will say. Rejoice." That was in the context of an argument. When everything seems hopeless, remember the hope in the Lord. More than that, Paul says to remember that you both are sisters for all eternity. If there is a deep issue, present all your anxieties to God who will help!

▼ **Romans 15:17**. When someone is feeling upset about certain practices of another, or deeply concerned with the failings of another, remember that Christ has welcomed you into His kingdom. He put up with the failings of the weak; He did not please Himself but rather sacrificed His own wishes to deal with those who were mistaken in their beliefs and practices. If we remember this, we too can put up with our spouses' failings or weaknesses.

▼ **1 Corinthians 11:21-27**. The situation here is one group of people thinking they are better or more deserving than another group of people. But when we take communion we are reminded that we are all sinners, deserving nothing, yet given grace and built up in the body of Christ. I was once told the story of a pastor who, before giving Holy Communion, would request that if anyone had issues with another member of the congregation to reconcile now, as the sign of being 'one body', otherwise they would eat and drink judgement on themselves. For years no one did anything, until at one service, suddenly a man ran across the hall to sit next to a woman. The pastor found out later that he had had a prolonged argument with his wife the week before, and now decided to resolve it immediately so as not to have judgement on himself!

There are many more reasons for reconciliation.

Conflict is not peculiar to marriage, but marriage makes conflict inescapable and with much more dire consequences. Conflict happens by definition when two different people are trying to come together to be or do something. It is a necessary process of working through those differences.

But what we need in conflict is often not the 'how' to resolve things. Instead, we need a *reason* to resolve things. And that is where the gospel in Scripture has many, many answers. The best way to handle conflict in marriage is to grow in maturity as Christians – to become more like Jesus Christ.

As we grow more aware of the welcome of God, the forgiveness of God, the hope of the gospel, the grace of God, and ultimately the love of God seen and experienced through our own personal relationship with Jesus Christ, we will be able to solve any problem, any difference that comes our way, whether in church or in our marriage.

After all… "*love covers a multitude of sins*" (1 Peter 4:8b).

And that, I think, is the key to conflict resolution.

APPENDIX B
MAYBE NOT?

"Wow… You mean this is what marriage is like? Then I don't want to get married!"

Perhaps some of you are thinking such thoughts at this moment. It is true – God's pattern of marriage is no joke! After all, when Jesus explained to His disciples that divorce is not an option in marriage and that we've got to stick it out, serving one another all the way till death, this was their response:

> *The disciples said to him, "If such is the case of a man with his wife, it is better not to marry."*
> *(Matthew 19:1)*

Yeah, even they were freaked out by it!

So what happens if we're not ready for marriage?

Some people will opt for loose relationships or cohabitation. But as we've seen, these do not reflect the pattern of marriage that God has set up. By not reflecting who God is, they are not honouring to God. These relationships are often quite disastrous in the long run, especially to our spiritual lives, and it is likely we will end up frustrated and alone.

Some will opt for singleness. This is a valid Scriptural option. There are people who remain single because of circumstances or past trauma, and others stay single by choice.

But let's keep in mind that being single is not an excuse for avoiding sacrificial relationships. In fact, many early Christians opted to be single because they could serve God and their neighbours much better without having to be 'burdened' by marriage.[1] They remained single so that they could focus on the one True Marriage better!

If we're not ready for marriage I believe the answer is to realise that we need more spiritual maturity first. It may mean that we don't have the mental framework of service and self-sacrifice that is required for marriage and children just yet. So take the time to grow, learn the Way of Jesus, and train in service through your local church ministries. If you are not sure, ask someone more mature, and listen to their assessment of your maturity.

All that said, when you think you are finally ready, take courage and go for it!

ENDNOTES

Chapter 1: Things Change
1. Wikipedia contributors, "Divorce in the United States," *Wikipedia*, http://en.wikipedia.org/wiki/Divorce_in_the_United_States#Rates_of_divorce.
2. Office for National Statistics, "Short Report: Cohabitation in the UK, 2012," http://www.ons.gov.uk/ons/rel/family-demography/families-and-households/2012/cohabitation-rpt.html.
3. "Marriage Dissolution Rates Up in Singapore," *Channel NewsAsia*, 6 April 2015, http://www.channelnewsasia.com/news/singapore/marriage-dissolution/1768390.html.
4. Government of Singapore, "Number of Marriages and Divorces," *Singapore Department of Statistics*, 29 July 2014, http://www.singstat.gov.sg/statistics/visualising-data/charts/number-of-marriages-and-divorces.

Chapter 2: The 113 Pattern
1. Michael Reeves, *The Good God* (Milton Keynes, UK: Paternoster, 2012), 28.
2. John Piper, *This Momentary Marriage* (Nottingham, UK: Inter-Varsity Press, 2009), 24.

Chapter 3: Rules of Engagement
1. Aelred of Rievaulx, *Spiritual Friendship: The Classic Text with a Spiritual Commentary by Dennis Billy, C.Ss.R.* (Notre Dame, IN: Ave Maria Press, 2008), 40–41.
2. Genesis 16
3. See, for example, Genesis 24:63.
4. With reference to Sinatra's popular hit, "My Way".
5. Glen Scrivener, "Marriage Course Handout 1," *Christ the Truth*, 1 February 2010, http://christthetruth.net/2010/02/01/marriage-course-handout-1.

6. John Piper, *This Momentary Marriage* (Nottingham, UK: Inter-Varsity Press, 2009), 25.
7. Glen Scrivener, "Marriage Course Handout 1," *Christ the Truth*, 1 February 2010, http://christthetruth.net/2010/02/01/marriage-course-handout-1.
8. John Piper, *This Momentary Marriage* (Nottingham, UK: Inter-Varsity Press, 2009), 25–26.
9. *Singaporean of the Day*, "The Devoted Husband," 8 February 2013, http://vimeo.com/59216632.
10. Jared C. Wilson, "The Bridegroom's Incredible Vow," *The Gospel Coalition*, 22 August 2014, http://thegospelcoalition.org/blogs/gospeldrivenchurch/2014/08/22/the-bridegrooms-incredible-vow.
11. That's a joke, by the way.
12. Glen Scrivener, "Marriage Course Handout 1," *Christ the Truth*, 1 February 2010, http://christthetruth.net/2010/02/01/marriage-course-handout-1.
13. Jared C. Wilson, "The Bridegroom's Incredible Vow," *The Gospel Coalition*, 22 August 2014, http://thegospelcoalition.org/blogs/gospeldrivenchurch/2014/08/22/the-bridegrooms-incredible-vow.

Chapter 4: When Two Become One (I)

1. *Jerry Maguire* is a movie made in 1996.
2. So why did they make humanity? We'll find out later!
3. See Genesis 29:25.
4. Wikipedia contributors, "2 Become 1," *Wikipedia*, http://en.wikipedia.org/wiki/2_Become_1.
5. Timothy Keller with Kathy Keller, *The Meaning of Marriage* (London, UK: Hodder & Stoughton, 2011), 134
6. Timothy Keller, "You Never Marry the Right Person," 5 January 2012, http://www.relevantmagazine.com/life/relationship/features/27749-you-never-marry-the-right-person.
7. Based on a story often told by a fellow pastor.
8. I wrote extensively about this subject in my other book, *The Plate Spinner* (Singapore: Graceworks, 2014).

Chapter 5: When Two Become One (II)

1. Romans 1:5.
2. Except, of course, for your personal relationship with Jesus.
3. Too bad this law doesn't apply for Singapore's National Service call-ups.
4. Technically speaking your relationship with God should be the number one priority – but you know what I mean!
5. By the way, "cleaving" in old English means "joining to", not "cutting away" (like the modern cleaver!).
6. David W. F. Wong, *Love's Rough Journeys* (Malaysia: Good News Resources, 1998), 34.
7. Can you see why Jesus said in Luke 14:26 that you must hate everyone else and love Him more? This is not a command to abandon them. It is a question of priorities – will you listen to Him more than the others? It will be equivalent to hating them and loving Him!
8. Co-Curricular Activity.
9. More about this in the next chapter.
10. 1 Corinthians 7:1–5.
11. Ann Voskamp, "Dear Kids: Why Wait Till Marriage – What No One Tells You & What I Wish Someone Had Told Me," *A Holy Experience*, 5 September 2014, http://www.aholyexperience.com/2014/09/dear-kids-why-wait-till-marriage-what-no-one-tells-you-what-i-wish-someone-had-told-me.
12. One Singaporean pastor recommended couples to have sex at least 2–3 times a week!
13. As often quoted by my senior pastor.
14. Glen Scrivener, "In Covenant Union, Other-Love is Self-Love but Self-Love is Not Other-Love," *Christ the Truth*, 13 December 2012, http://christthetruth.net/2012/09/13/in-covenant-union-other-love-is-self-love-but-self-love-is-not-other-love.
15. Michael Reeves, *The Good God* (Milton Keynes, UK: Paternoster, 2012), 30–31.
16. Glen Scrivener, "Interlocking Neuroses," *Christ the Truth*, 4 January 2010, http://christthetruth.wordpress.com/2010/01/04/interlocking-neuroses.

17. This could be manifested in any number of ways – serving the less fortunate, ministering to orphans, helping the emotionally drained, etc.

Chapter 6: A Dance for Two

1. 1 Corinthians 12.
2. For example, John 5:20.
3. 1 Corinthians 12:4.
4. A title of a book by Arthur F. Miller, Jr (Grand Rapids: Zondervan, 1999).
5. Glen Scrivener, *321: The Story of God, the World and You* (Leyland, UK: 10Publishing, 2014), 166.
6. Glen Scrivener, *321: The Story of God, the World and You* (Leyland, UK: 10Publishing, 2014), 163.
7. However, no one is doubting the ability of women to fight in Mixed Martial Arts.
8. As noted in a series of lectures by Larry Crabb.
9. Genesis 3:16 (also refer to Genesis 4:7 to see the meaning of 'desire' here)
10. Implying the old categories of treating people differently because of intellect, race, nationality, gender, etc.
11. H. Norman Wright, *The Premarital Counseling Handbook* (Chicago, IL: Moody Publishers, 1992).
12. John Piper and Wayne Grudem, *Recovering Biblical Manhood and Womanhood* (Wheaton, IL: Crossway, 1991).
13. Glen Scrivener, "The Role of Marital Roles," *Christ the Truth*, 12 August 2012, http://christthetruth.net/2012/08/12/the-role-of-marital-roles.
14. I'm using the biblical sense of the word "jealous", which is wanting the very best for her above everyone else.
15. At the end of Matthew 5, Jesus implies that if your enemy wants to do something cruel to you, do more than what he says – and this will show him the glory of God.
16. Strange, isn't it, that fish works the other way?

Chapter 7: The Final Word

1. See 1 Corinthians 7:27-35. In fact, much of the early post-New Testament church advocated the single life dedicated to God far above marriage, wherever possible!

2. E.g. Mark 12:25.

Appendix A: Conflict Resolution
1. If you didn't get it, it's a pun on 'becoming hysterical'.

Appendix B: Maybe Not?
1. 1 Corinthians 7:33.